How to Hygge Your Summer

(How to have a fun and hyggely time all year round)

By Jo Kneale

Copyright

**This book is dedicated
with much love
To my Mum and Dad
who have always believed in me
and loved me.**

About the Author

Jo Kneale has been a teacher, a mother, a teacher again, a teaching assistant and now an Office Ninja for her husband's law firm, Peter Kneale Solicitor. She's been good at hygge since she can remember, but only had a word for it in the last five years, when an unhealthy obsession with The Killing led to a fascination with all things Danish and a love of the concept of hygge.

Married for nearly 24 years to Peter, she has three teenage children and seven guinea pigs at the moment. She likes to read, watch Game of Thrones and West Wing, visit cities with her husband and take part in TV quiz shows. Three to date, including The Chase where she won an amazing £47,000 by herself but had to share with the rest of the team, bringing home £20,000. That was a good day.

She's always wanted to write a book, and writing about hygge is what she does almost daily on her blog, How to Hygge the British Way. Her first book, 50 Ways to Hygge the British Way, was published in March 2017 and her third book, Hashtag Hygge, is currently in production. Both are or will be available from Amazon in Kindle and paperback form.

Jo believes that everybody can enjoy more hygge in their lives, they just have to recognise it, own it and hashtag it.

If you're interested in learning more about Jo's style of British Hygge, then visit the website, www.howtohyggethebritishway.com or join The Hygge Nook group on Facebook.

Thanks go to....

The many members of The Hygge Nook who helped me with ideas for the book including (but not limited to):-

Sasha Toby, Sarah Carlson, Lis Harwood, Nikki Read, Samantha Varnam, Ruth Mackay Langford, Sarah Wilks, Trudie Benney, Helen Ward, Kayleigh Tanner, Nicky Jones, Mel Gulliford, Shellye Carpenter, Lori Ellen Holcombe, Alison Mizon, Suzanne Tappenden, Cynthia Jane Martz, Kathryn Jaggard, Angie Stokes, Barbara Allen, Robbin Dee, Jill Leontiadis, Nicky Dunne Gowdy, Louise M Bridgwater, Nicola Kendrick, Melissa Brown, Sue De Chaneet, M J Bujold, Fleur Pearson, Carly McCarty, Kimberly Poe Hunt, Joanne Chapman, Claire Gifford, DeAnn Malone, Michele Dunn, Kimmy Harding, Noel Minneci, Amy Bull Snr, Justin Williams, Cassandra Scrutton, Andrea Isaacs Durlak, Kathryn Bostock-Williams, Nancy Krost Christensen, Eileen Lavender.

Contents

Introduction

There comes a point when you must cast off the blankets, swap the cups of tea for cooling lemonade and even the most die-hard Winter hygge fans have to admit that hibernation is over and the brief season known as Summer is upon us.

Many who fail to totally grasp the idea that hygge is a feeling and not a set of props find the idea of summer hygge sounds bizarre... how can you hygge with no cushions, no candles, no roaring fire? Isn't that the whole point of hygge?

Well, no. Not really. Hygge isn't a seasonal thing, it's an all-year thing, because it's not the cold nights in or slurps of hot drinks that are hygge. It's what lies between and around. The nebulous feelings of warmth, safety, welcome, togetherness and belonging that are there in the wintertime, yes... but equally as valid in the depths of summer, when time stands still and light lasts much longer. Don't believe me? Read on.... And discover how hygge; British, Danish or whatever, can be found even in the sunniest of spots.

Firstly, though, let's remember what hygge actually means.

Hygge in its purest form is simply about togetherness and appreciating life.

BronteAurell

www.howtohyggethebritishway.com

Trust Brontë Aurell[1] to sum up hygge in a simple sentence. Actually, I do trust her to. This is the lady who said on her website (and in Time Out London) "Do you know who is really good at hygge? Like, really good at it? The British. Down a nice pub, sitting down, talking around the table and taking time out. You've been doing hygge all along. And when you think about it like that, hygge suddenly makes sense. That is where it is and that is what it means, inside the space where you feel happy. If it isn't the pub, it might be a café, your kitchen, a bedsit, a mansion or a tent in a field: hygge is always inside you."

---

[1] Bronte is a Dane married to a Swede who owns and runs Scandinavian Kitchen, a beautifully hyggely café, in London. Her books on Hygge are well worth reading, full of recipes and wisdom.

We've been doing hygge all along, get it? And that hygge is not the stuff that comes with a label saying hygge, but the feeling we get in a place of greater safety. That when we find a spot on this planet that makes us feel safe, we will be able to spend time there in peace, happily alone or in company and with a security in ourselves that everywhere we go, we always take the hygge.

Hygge, most simply, is a way of looking at and feeling about life. It's an appreciation of the lovely things in life, both human and inanimate. It's about appreciating what we have and sharing that with others. It's about creating a safe space where people can get together and be confident that they won't be criticised, won't feel isolated, won't be afraid to share their thoughts and feelings as long as they are prepared to accept everybody else in the same spirit.

Hygge works best in a place where the people agree, for the sake of unity, to set aside any differences in race, religion, politics or football and agree (even if only by tacit consent) not to mention anything that might cause ill-feeling. It works because they agree to honour their common humanity at that point in time and space, and to focus on the things that keep us bound together as humans, rather than the things that separate us as tribes.

At this point I have to give a massive shout out to my virtual hygge friends: all the people who belong to The Hygge Nook[2] on Facebook and who were always ready with a suggestion, willing to read over parts and point out the problems and, in several cases, to let me use their photographs. I love this group, and they give me my daily hygge fix at a time when the mainstream media have turned their back on it, because they don't see it as a 'summer thing'.

And hygge has a real focus on the simple, the easy, the basic. It's not about luxury, so put that champagne back on the shelf and get the elderflower cordial out! It's not about having or doing the best, being the most unique. It's about making the most of what we have, and sharing that with others. And that works so well in the summer. What could taste better than the first strawberries from your own garden? How about sharing them with your friend or neighbour? How simple is a walk along the beach? An afternoon in the park? Playing water fights with balloons and squeezy bottles? Hygge doesn't need to cost anything more than time and smiles.

---

[2] https://www.facebook.com/groups/TheHyggeNook/

2017 (as I write this) is the first proper summer of hygge since the Great Danish Invasion of 2016. It will be a damn shame if hygge gets put in a box at the end of April and perhaps comes out again in October. As well as a waste of perfectly beautiful hyggering time. And yet, if you really are still unsure how to separate the throws from the feeling, then there is a proper risk that you won't bring the hygge with you.

All I ask of you during this book is to keep an open mind, and cast aside any prejudice you have against the idea of hygge as an open-air activity. Hygge is a year-long feeling. Meik Wiking said so, Brontë says so and I, British Hygge Jem, say so as well.

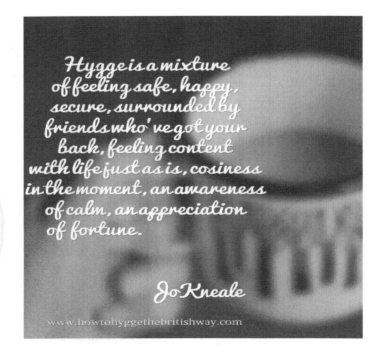

Hygge is a mixture of feeling safe, happy, secure, surrounded by friends who've got your back, feeling content with life just as is, cosiness in the moment, an awareness of calm, an appreciation of fortune.

Jo Kneale

www.howtohyggethebritishway.com

What this book isn't:

Despite the title, this book isn't a prescriptive list of things you must do to be hyggely in summertime. It probably makes suggestions rather than commands, gives examples of my own summer hygge and ideas gleaned from friends, family and the Hygge Nook. Nothing costs a great deal, everything should be accessible to most people.

It isn't about having a perfect house or lifestyle either. Hygge is so incredibly personal that trying to tie it down to one lifestyle or decorating trend would be madness.

What I hope this book is:

I hope this book is an inspiration to you. I hope it gets you thinking about what hygge is to you, and how you can build that hygge into many parts of your life.

I hope you will look around your home and garden with love and work out how to use it to the best effect. I hope you look at your life and lifestyle and examine it closely for hygge moments that you can enjoy.

Most of all I hope you get a real sense of gratitude, whatever your situation, and carry that gratitude with you throughout the summer and into Autumn when, doubtlessly, I'll have written another book and we can settle down for some good winter hygge.

Homework:

I wanted this book to be a lot more interactive than my last book, so I'm giving you homework. If you've bought the Kindle version, then you'll need a notepad and pen or pencils. If you've bought the paperback, then there are pages included to scribble over and make notes on. Either way, when you see the heading **Your Homework**, be prepared to do a little bit of thinking and listing. The tasks are designed to get you thinking about what summer hygge will mean for you as an individual, so there really are no right or wrong answers.

And first off, if you're on Facebook go and join The Hygge Nook[3], or find me on Twitter and Instagram. I love meeting new people and the conversations we have there will also encourage you to think of your life in a more hyggely way.

I hope you enjoy the chance to think through your hygge!

---

[3] https://www.facebook.com/groups/TheHyggeNook/ Again... I can't stress how good these people are!

Hygge in the Garden

Do you remember the long hot days of summer when you were little? The days when your Mum would throw a packet of crisps and a bottle of water at you and tell you to stay out for as long as possible? Do you remember the mad bike rides up and down the road, trying to do wheelies with a mate standing on the back wheel? Did you ever spend hours sat on the parched grass trying desperately to make a grass stem whistle?

I was born in 1968 (no, don't work out my age) so when Britain had its best and longest heatwave in 1976 I was 8 years old. Old enough to know this was unusual. There were ladybirds everywhere; we had brown, parched grass, no hosepipes allowed anywhere and a desperate need to find a space to keep cool.

We sat in the shade of any and every tree on the school field that year. Even the little sapling just planted. As long as it was a shadow, we sat there. And I remember long afternoons spent just being. I'm sure we did some school work... I think... but I don't remember it. Just turning cartwheels and hoping that Mum would have a couple of ten pence pieces so we could buy a sour lemonade lolly from the ice cream van now and again.

And when we did get home it was back outside again. Into our undies (swimming clothes if we were patient enough) and into the smallest paddling pool ever. Seriously. It was a washing up bowl. But it filled up with less than a bucket of water saved from the bath and we could splash only until that was gone, when we made like lions, and slumped in the shade again.

Summer hygge happens for the most part outside. As long as it's not raining, we move our lives outside and enjoy both sun and shadow until the golden light gleams through the branches and somebody finally realises it's time to go in.

This chapter on hygge in the garden is divided into three: structural hygge, hygge with children and hygge with adults.

Structural hygge is about the things you can do or build to make your garden hyggely, the areas of a garden that lend themselves to hygge or the products that will enhance the hygge in the garden.

Hygge with Children is self-explanatory. These are the activities and hygge moments that happen best with children, or at least those of a younger mindset.

Hygge with Adults explores the more adult side of hygge. There is a great recipe included here; a wicked idea for ice lollies that are totally not for sharing!

Structural Hygge

Question: You have a garden or a yard, where you sit or play most of the summer. It's got a patch of grass, quite scuffed where the ball ends up time and again, and you have a couple of fabric deckchairs that come out of the garage for you to sit on now and again. Usually you just throw a blanket down on the ground.

Or your garden is massive, with a seating area and a cooking area. The solar powered lights make it a pleasure to hang around in the evenings, and a mosquito repellent means that the pesky flies keep away.

Which is most hyggely? I'll give you the answer at the end of the chapter.

Structural hygge as I use it means anything in and of the garden that is designed to enhance hygge, so it's the bones of the garden. The furniture, the accessories and generally most things that you can spend your money on at the Garden Centre or DIY store any weekend between Easter and August, when it changes over to leaf blowers and Christmas decorations. It's worth looking at how the garden is arranged as well, as there are definitely some hard landscape features that can encourage you to have more hyggely times in the garden.

An Outdoor Room.

This doesn't mean a whole outdoor room, it means an area that, with a little bit of work, can be ready to use as an outdoor room. It could be a decking area, or a patio. Any space where you can assemble either a place to eat or a place to sit in a few minutes and where you can stay happily for hours. It's well worth considering wind, light and distance from the house in this. Too windy and you won't want to sit out, too sunny and the middle of the day will feel like an oven. You are searching for the mythical Goldilocks point in the garden; not too hot, not too cold, just right. Mine is an area under the trees about 5 metres from my living room French windows. I had it set up as an arbour for one brief shining season, until the first winter storm ripped my roof to pieces. It's perfectly useable without cover, but I wanted an all-year area to sit out in the snow and roast marshmallows over the fire-pit. I am working on getting another, stronger roof up.

It's worth considering the materials underfoot carefully. We have patio stones, which are easy to clean with a power washer every other year, but can be both rough and cold underfoot on a cool day. One of my brothers has a decking area, which feels warmer to bare feet, but has a habit of growing green, slippery slime and needing more regular maintenance. I also worry about splinters. Yet another area of my garden has stone chippings, which look lovely at first but need the bits picking out by hand to maintain the beach look and are also very hard on feet.

Don't be afraid to strip off your shoes and socks in the garden or builder's supplier to walk on whatever surface you're contemplating. Like the carpet in the living room, you need this to be right for you.

You should also carefully consider what the main purpose of the area is. Are you great eaters *al fresco*? Will you want a table and chairs to be your main feature? Or are you more inclined to sit around a fire pit into the early hours talking? It is possible to have both, with clever use of space and furniture that's been well designed, but if you only have one small area to use, then think carefully.

We have a sunny eating area and a shaded sitting area in the garden. That way we can sit out to eat as soon as the sun makes an appearance, rather than waiting for the heat of a summer's day. When the kids were little and I wasn't working full time, I often used to take my coffee out there on a spring morning just to hear the wind and the birds and the traffic noise....

Our seating area, beneath the trees, has a cheap metal settee and armchair set. They're not the height of luxury, but they're a good depth and size for all people and, with judicious use of cushions, they're comfy enough to sit on all night long.

The ultimate in outside rooms would, of course, be a summer house or outside building. Not a shed, though, unless you are really good at making something from nothing. I'm thinking more a glass and wood construction, with doors that open wide and a wall that lets in plenty of light to the inside. There are a load of summer house ideas on Pinterest, some painted and some plain. I love the little spaces that have been set up as outside rooms, with seats, cushions and rugs. The summerhouse belongs to a lovely Hygge Nook member, who sets it up every April and uses it often.

Summer houses mean that you can always hygge outside, even in the rain or on a breezy day. Imagine a little tea tray on a table with some homemade biscuits, as you and a couple of friends nibble and sip while outside the gentlest of summer

showers scatters cooling rain over the lawn. Or, more likely with me, a mug of hot chocolate, for even in summer hygge there is space for cocoa, while you curl up in the chair and read a good murder story. Agatha Christie's Evil Under the Sun is excellent summer murder fare.

Investing in the summer house might take money, amount to be discussed between you and your conscience, but what you do with it then only needs ingenuity and elbow grease. A few tins of paint, some material, items borrowed from the house just for the summer needn't cost that much. And think of the two hyggely weekend celebrations you could have for the official opening and closing of the summer house and garden.

---

[4] A Perfect Summerhouse: this one actually belongs to a Hygge Nook member, Kathryn Bostock-Williams, who has let me use the photo in the book. Thank you, Kathryn!

If you can't afford a summerhouse, then improvise. Cheap fabric gazebos are available during the summertime. Set it up, furnish underneath with things that you can carry in and out as the need flows and for less than £100 you can have a fake summerhouse to sit under. Not pretty, but practical. Christina Strutt[5], of Cabbages and Roses, often sets up an outdoor room this way.

Lighting the outdoor space

Any outdoor seating area needs to work well in daylight and evening hours. Looking at what lighting you want or can have is a help. Will you be happy enough in the gloaming[6] by the light of a fire? Do you need candles or fairy lights to help? Is there an outdoor plug available or will you be relying on battery operated lights to give you the soft glow of a hygge corner? You're not doomed to choose one and stick with it, you can mix and match as much as you like. I find a good combination of them all helps. The fire will eventually start to die down whilst still pumping out a fair amount of heat, while candles stood in hurricane jars look pretty and work for keeping the flame safe.

---

[5]   http://www.express.co.uk/life-style/style/482227/Cabbage-Roses-founder-Christina-Strutt

[6] Isn't gloaming a wonderful word? I first read it in Jane Eyre, and had to look it up. It's from the Old English word for dusk, or sunset.

I don't have an outdoor plug, so I find solar lights an absolute boon. These gather their energy during daylight hours and then release it as gentle lights during the darkness. You can find all sorts of shapes and sizes, and very often the cheaper stores such as Poundland or B & M (in the UK) have offers on, so they needn't cost a fortune. The solar powered lightbulb lights below were available in early summer for a pound each… that's a garden lit gently for a tenner!

Of course, you can always use the hygge-lover's favourite, tealights, to add the candle light. I use empty *Bonne Maman* conserve jars and thick garden wire to make a handle. We have some iron 'sticks' that I think once had a job holding tape around roadworks and things… they work well for suspending jar lights from, so that's what they do. I'm always fiddling with the lighting in the garden, finding what suits and what works best. This year I want a curtain of fairy lights behind the seating area, in and between the ivy walls we have there, but for that I need to organise an external plug. There's always another job to do!

And related to light, we come to citronella candles. Any time spent outside can be made less comfortable by the presence of mosquitos or other biting insects. You really don't need to worry if you have me with you, I'm like a magnet for them. You'll be safe and I'll be a red mess the next day, but that's okay.

I try a lot of things to keep them away from me, including Jungle Formula insect repellent, but I also light copious amounts of candles with either citronella or lavender scents, both of which are supposed to keep the biters at bay.

Good citronella candles are hard to find, but it's worth asking friends which ones they have that work well. They should make the place a little less pleasant for flying friends.

Heating choices

If you are going to spend any time outside before May and after September, it is well worth considering a heating source. This (like everything in hygge) is a matter of personal choice and financial capability.

Fire-pits are available for £30 and upwards. They're like metal basins in which you make and light the fire. You can use charcoal or wood, but be prepared to spend some time learning how to set a fire and how to damp down the fire at the end of the night.

Chimneas cost slightly more but look prettier on the patio. Also, the flames are contained rather than open to the outside so it may be a safer option if you have younger children or wear a lot of flowing clothes. Again, knowing how to set a fire well is a necessity. My brother has a chimnea and it's good to sit next to, but I miss the sight of the flames.

Patio heaters can be run on gas or electric, and prices can vary enormously. There is also a wide variety of styles, so you should be able to find something that suits your house style. Consider the cost of the fuel as well as the initial spend. Gas heaters tend to cost more initially, but I haven't investigated which have cheaper running costs.

I have a fire-pit, which I love, but I know I would never even have considered it just three years ago. My children are aged 15 upwards, so I'm trusting them to be sensible around the open flame. It is lovely, though, and as close to a real fire as we get in our house, so I'm determined to make the most of it over the summer months.

The warmth of an outdoor fire will extend any hygge in the garden, making it possible to sit out earlier and later in the year and for a longer period of time.

Water features in the garden

There is something so relaxing about the sound of running water. It's one of the favourite sounds featured on Meditation tapes. It also makes me want to pee when I first hear it, but if I can get past that, I find it relaxing.

I also love watching the effect that sunlight has on water, with the reflections and the rainbows that can be created. Light and water go well together.

Getting water into your garden can be as easy as having an upturned bin lid that the birds use as a bird bath, to installing an all-singing, all-dancing fountain that will gently burble as you sip your wine. All I can keep saying is that hygge is not about spending a lot of money, so if you can make a water feature without breaking the bank, then go for it.

In my first married home, some of my best hygge was to be had watching the birds in the birdbath... a cheap concrete affair... that I had carefully placed so that the sun hit it in the early Spring mornings. Watching the water being sprayed upwards was a welcome pause from the dishwashing, and a beautiful picture that defied capture in a camera but lives forever in my memory. The birdbath cost me about £30 in total. I have seen the same effect from a wide, shallow dish on a length of pipe... not pretty, but very cost-effective.

The feature above uses old buckets and watering cans to make a unique talking point for the garden.

Small water features can be found from £20.00 upwards, with the price rising as the size increases. Moving water is best, since it will keep fresher than still water, and a small table top feature can always be included in a garden space or summer house.

Ponds and pools are also very hyggely to watch, although the installation and upkeep may not be! I am no garden designer, so I'd be very wrong to dictate on size or shape to you. Ask someone who knows, either professional or very good amateur. The size and position of the pond will decide what you can put in it, I understand, with shallow ponds in full sun being dangerous for fish and frogs. Do your research, and plan it well. What I think you're aiming for is a pond that encourages wildlife, so that you get a neat little ecosystem, with fish, frogs, insects and birds.

A paddling pool will probably not look beautiful, but during the summer it can be a source of fun and hygge. Look into possible costs and my advice would be to buy as big as you can, as long as you know how to care for it.

7

Building in shade in the garden is useful advice. There will come a day when sitting in the full sun is just too darned hot, and then a little shade, either full or dappled, will be a pleasant

---

[7] This picture is, of course, Versailles. An example of what you can achieve if money's no object!

sensation. Trees are wonderful shade providers, but do take up a lot of space. Parasols or canopies can be put up or down according to the light, and many are available in a range of colours so that, whatever the colour scheme of the garden there should be a shade to match.

You can get free standing parasols or ones that attach to a hanging hook, so that the stand is off to one side and doesn't take up valuable sitting space. Prices vary, so do shop around and check you get good value.

My parents have a roll-out canopy fixed to the side of their South-facing patio doors. That's really useful for giving a little shade to the inside room as well. Good ones start from £150.00 depending on width.

The picture opposite shows a good use of shade, with that provided by the lean-to against the house being enhanced by the large parasol. And comfortable chairs will keep you there for hours.

When the children were small, we spent many afternoons making our own shades, with blankets and sheets across poles or rope. Setting up the den took almost as long as sitting in it lasted, before they were off to play and explore again, but in a good spell we could leave the dens there overnight and play the next day. They were useful spaces for colouring or reading.

Whatever solution you choose, use it well. In the heat of a summer's day the shade it casts may be the most pleasant thing you find to sit and eat in. Have the shade and seating close together, and easy to move.

Building in a sun trap can be a good idea as well. By this, I mean a place that gets the sun with none of the wind. It's lovely to sit out on mild days, but even in June there can be a breeze in parts that ruffles hair and makes reading harder. Having a warm, sunny spot that is closed off and gets very little wind expands the sitting season. You can use the barriers in the garden already, or use landscaping features such as fence panels or judicious planting to make the sun trap more effective. Of course, you would never sit out in the Sun for too long without ensuring you have adequate sun protection. Sunburn isn't funny.

A play area in the garden. I like having different areas of the garden, using different materials according to the purpose. For many years of child-rearing, we had an area under the trees that was specifically designed as a play area. It had the swing and the small climbing frame that my pre-schoolers used every dry day.

The hard standing for a play house was there as well, but we never actually got the wooden playhouse of my dreams, using instead a small Little Tike's house that we bought for £20 off a friend. Beyond a brush over and a couple of loads of replacement play bark, the area looked after itself. Did it look beautiful? No, except to the children who visited and loved the fact that even on a damp day there was an area in the garden to play out in.

Hygge with the Kids

I now have three teenagers, but believe me I have been through years of being a mother entertaining children in the garden! I refer you back to the Structural Hygge chapter and the part about a play area. We had a play area for the first 13 years in this house, and it made getting out and playing whatever the weather much easier. Because it was contained as well, it made tidy up time quicker.

Children love spending time in their own garden, especially when the weather is too hot to venture far, or they are just old enough to want to be out of sight and too young to trust anywhere too far away. Giving them freedom with a boundary helps them to feel more grown up without actually putting them in any true danger. Set your rules as to where they can and can't go, what they can and cannot touch, and as long as your garden has been childproofed with tools, chemicals etc. safely locked away then you can let them play with minimal interruption and regular peeps to make sure they're safe.

Spending time in greenery is an important part of summer hygge. There is often a more relaxed feel to time spent outside, and a feeling of timelessness. Children, during their long summer holidays, have a great ability to lose track of time. Days roll on in endless fun, and only those mean things called Parents put an end to it with the clarion call for Bed. One of my Hygge Nook friends calls it being un-calendared. No appointments, no need to do anything. Just days of being. Pure hygge.

Bliss was it in that dawn to be alive, But to be young was very heaven!

William Wordsworth

www.howtohyggethebritishway.com

Eating outside with the children. We used to often leave the door open to the garden for a majority of the day. The garden faces South, and often at lunchtime I would encourage the children to sit out on the step and eat their sandwich or cake. The crumbs were easier to clean, the children enjoyed eating to the sound of bird song (and the constant traffic sound from the road behind the wall) and I loved knowing that they were getting their Vitamin D from a natural source and not a pill.

They also talked to each other when they ate, especially on the days when I treated it as basically a proper family meal, with juice, cutlery and full table set. Any meal is always a chance for hygge, and starting them early is no bad thing.

Eating presents problems, though, in terms of wasps and flies. We never absolutely solved either, but we did find that wasp traps worked both for luring the stinging things away from the table and for capturing them. Traps can be made for free from old plastic bottles[8] or, if the aesthetics don't suit, glass traps can be bought from £10 upwards.

We always had plastic melamine plates to eat off with the children, and as a family in the garden. There are some pretty, colourful patterns out there, they go in the dishwasher and they don't break easily. They are also lightweight and easy to pack for an outing or picnic. There are very few things more civilised than eating your picnic butties off a plate.

The children need to be trained to bring their rubbish in when they're finished. Bits of food left out are unsightly and can attract the attention of less desirable residents.

---

[8] http://www.wikihow.com/Make-a-Wasp-Trap

Using the children to water the garden. The garden, if it has any sort of flower or plant in, will need watering during the longest, hottest summer weather. I found that the children actually enjoyed this task on hot summer days, and that they didn't mind whether it was being done by a hosepipe or watering cans, as long as I was prepared for as much water to go over their legs, backs and fronts as on the plants.

We had cheap plastic watering cans, one each, and they each got a can of water to use up on the plants. Using the hosepipe was more problematic because they argued over who got first use. I found that the sprinkler was a good thing here, and that once I set it up, I could putter in the garden while the three of them went mad jumping in and over and through the water. Laughter is so good for hygge, don't you think?

Water play in general is excellent hygge. As long as nobody throws water intentionally to hurt other people, getting wet and cooling down is good fun for adults and children alike. I have found some excellent water play activities on Babble.com[9] and happyhooligans.ca[10] that would make excellent hygge, building memories, cooling anybody within the vicinity, and

---

[9]   https://www.babble.com/toddler/25-fun-toddler-activities-for-the-summer-bucket-list/ I love the homemade sprinkler! I know I'm an adult, but I'm making one of those this year!

[10] http://happyhooligans.ca/25-water-play-ideas-backyard/

keeping children occupied in the garden. When I think back to my children's days at home, I really appreciate the long lengths of time they made me stop and play. Now I have fantastic memories of their faces (and my wet t shirts) and the feeling of contentment that comes from a day of fun in the sun. I think pre-schoolers especially have a sense of natural hygge that we as adults need to rediscover. Water play, fun as it is for everybody, is a good place to find family hygge.

Again, your teenagers may squirm at the idea of watering the garden without payment, but they won't be able to resist joining in water fights. Using super-soakers, squeezy bottles, buckets of water and anything else to cool down sounds like child's play... and it is…. but play is fun for everyone. Organise teams, play catch the flag, be prepared for a lot of noise and set teenage boys or girls free for some mayhem. Now and again, it's such a release of pent up energy.

Saturday Night at the Movies

My daughter's friend celebrates her birthday in May. So do I, but I have never been as lucky as she was last year. Her rather beautiful idea was to hire a screen, borrow a projector and to have an outdoor cinema. Like everything in Britain, it was heavily reliant on the weather, but Fortune was on their side, so the evening was dry and warm enough with blankets spread out on the ground and they even moved a settee outside.

With popcorn, drinks and her parents acting as waiter and waitress for the food, the 10 teenage girls had a fine time. I know my daughter loved it, and would desperately love to do it for her birthday. Her birthday, it should be noted, is in February. There's very little chance we'll do an outside movie night for the date itself, but I'm thinking that a night to celebrate the end of GCSEs might be a good idea. With projector hire from as little as £25 and projectors available to buy from as little as £60, this could be a regular session.

I'm thinking…. Netflix movies played on the computer and sound surround via speakers moved outside. We have two very useful trees that could be used to support the screen (aka a sheet) and the rest of the lawn available for tiered seating from the blanket on the ground upwards. An age-appropriate series like A Series of Unfortunate Events screened outside for a small group of friends could make this summer a memorable one for all concerned. Think of the hygge they'd have, not only on the night itself but in the shared memories through the winter.

And to make the evening even more memorable, why not do as one of our Hygge Nook members does and set up a sundae bar? She writes, "We have make your own Sundae nights with the kids. We put out chocolate and vanilla ice cream containers and put out bananas, cherries, nuts, syrup, sprinkles, whipped cream, caramel and marshmallow toppings and you build your own sundae." Imagine watching the film with that sort of ice cream!

Outdoor play ideas. Sport in the garden and summer don't always go together. On rainy days, you may be stuck inside (see Rainy Day Hygge for ideas to counteract boredom) while really hot days don't encourage long hours chasing a ball or running around.

We find sports in the summer becomes an evening activity, when the heat of the day has passed and the family are lounging around outside. My daughter doesn't do *Still* well, so

she is only too ready to grab a Badminton racquet and shuttlecock to challenge her father to a game. The same with Frisbee or ball games: we tend to wait until the garden has cooled a little before getting the games out.

At the beginning and end of summertime, though, getting out and playing is certainly to be encouraged. With smaller children, the games should focus on building skills like balance, catching and throwing. Using buckets and plant pots as targets, and using any balls to hand builds skills for the pre-schooler while having fun at the same time. Learning through play, see? For brilliant outdoor play ideas for toddlers and early year's children, I found both notimeforflashcards.com[11]

---

[11]   http://www.notimeforflashcards.com/2012/03/50-simple-outdoor-activities-for-kids.html a list that possibly has something for everyone!

and popsugar.com[12] have extensive lists that use household objects or easily collected objects to encourage fun (and learning) in the sun.

For older children, the idea of 'sports' in the garden may not have the cachet it used to. The space is too limited, the company a bit hit and miss. For them, the idea of a Garden Gym may have more appeal. Using re-purposed items, it should be possible to exercise the body without leaving the yard. The website, Greatist.com[13] has some ideas designed for adults, but your teenagers will enjoy making and using them. Tyres and water bottles also provide cheap and easily obtained weights for building core muscles. Is body building hygge? Well, if it means everybody is together, laughing, active and enjoying each other's presence, then I'd argue it can be... especially if it's washed down with lemonade or ice cream shared as they pant together on the grass.

Since activity outside usually leads to dirty hands and dirty shoes, it may be sensible to have a cleaning off area just inside the door. A place for shoes to be left and with easy access to a basin for washing hands can help to keep the muck and inevitable grass cuttings in one place. The hygge won't last if you have to clean up after children every five minutes.

12   https://www.popsugar.com/moms/Outdoor-Activities-Kids-Summer-30688762

13   http://greatist.com/fitness/21-diy-gym-equipment-projects-make-home
Adults and teenagers can make a gym to use in the back garden. It's on my list this year!

The Best Water Slide Ever... Get some plastic sheeting, like a camping tarpaulin or poly sheeting from the garden centre, some cheap shampoo or washing up liquid and a sprinkling hose. Squirt the soap over the sheeting, keep it wet and watch them slide.

The Best Recipe for Kids in the Garden... Make your own lemonade. Take 6 lemons, pare the yellow skin off 3 of them very thinly using a zester or peeler, remove all the white pith from all 6 and squeeze the juice of all 6 into a bowl with the zest and 5oz of caster sugar. Pour over 2 ½ pints of boiling water, stir well, cover and leave overnight in a cool place. The next day, add more sugar to taste. Bottle into sterilised bottles with sterilised corks and then serve, either straight or diluted with fizzy water. You can also freeze the recipe to make ice pops.

Hygge for Adults

If you are a lucky adult who owns a garden and enjoys gardening... I mean, really enjoys it and thinks there are very few pleasures to compare to a day spent digging and mulching and manuring... well, I think you are a lucky person.

I love the idea of gardening, and adore grabbing Gardener's World on TV when I can (not the Friday evening show, but there is a mid-afternoon weekend showing now) but I am not green-fingered and really, the upkeep of the garden is a step beyond for me.

That's partly why I need a garden that either I am happy leaving wild (and we'll not talk about what might be hidden behind the bushes in it) or that has been carefully designed to be easy to care for. Not too many difficult plants, a care scheme that doesn't take too long and watering that is either done by a system (my Dad has one of those) or is a few pots around the back door and makes an enjoyable puttery moment for me.

I have to think hard about what plants I put in, for one thing. Nothing likely to grow too big, and nothing that requires frost cover during the winter. I love bedding plants because they're cheap and colourful, but I tend to keep them to pots by the patio so that watering isn't a whole garden affair. And some plants I choose specifically to be drought resistant. It helps when lavender is one of them. Beautiful, drought-resistant and a pretty smell? Triple winner!

You can find plenty of good advice on designing your own low maintenance garden online, or in several good books. It mustn't be fashionable at the moment, because all the books called Low Maintenance are older than 5 years and available secondhand on Amazon for a penny! It's mostly a case of looking at what surfaces you use in the garden, having a good system to deal with weeds and leaves, and being honest in your evaluation of how much time you actually have available to look after the garden. If you're like me, concentrate on getting flowers into pots only in the area where you sit. Or... like I hope to do later this year... pay for a gardener to maintain the area for you.

For the fortunate ones for whom gardening is a pleasure, I give you these wise words from a Hygge Nook member: "I love being in my garden tending to flowers and plants, cutting the grass and then sitting with a glass of something cold (booze not juice!) and enjoying my hard work to keep and maintain my space while smelling the fresh cut grass smell that's filled the air." There's a pure hygge moment by itself, after the work of maintenance comes the hygge of enjoyment. You have to do the work to deserve the reward!

Adults in the garden fall generally into two camps: either they are parents and have children to watch, or they are child-free and able to relax completely. Parents should refer to Hygge with the Kids above... and then read below to see what they can do when the little ones have gone to bed. Otherwise, treat your garden or outdoor space as a natural extension of the house, an extra room that you can use for at least 3 months a year. It's a ready-made entertainment area, because the clean up afterwards is much easier.

So, as an adult, what are you going to use the garden for? And what hygge can you expect to feel in it?

Cooking and eating al fresco is perhaps the most obvious way to 'get your hygge on' in the garden. Food and hygge go together, and there are few things more hyggely than having a few friends around and sharing food and drink with them. I could fill this book with recipes now, for salads, desserts, drinks and more besides. I won't, because that would be cheating. I can point you in the direction of Jamie Oliver's BBQ book[14] or The Barbecue! Bible by Steven Raichlen[15]. As books on barbecuing go, they both come highly recommended.

I know that there are gas or charcoal barbies and that sizes and prices can go from a few pounds up to thousands. Just buy the best one you can afford, and don't feel the need to be flash. Barbecues are really hygge, because the chances are that several people will help with the cooking, simply because there is something so enticing about cooking burgers or sausages that draws in the common or garden party-goer. Everybody has a trick or a useful piece of advice to give and gathering around a grill to chat and turn over the sausages is very hyggely.

---

[14] https://www.amazon.co.uk/Jamies-Food-Tube-Jamie-Olivers-ebook/dp/B00ZGUVM42/ref=sr_1_2?ie=UTF8&qid=1491330849&sr=8-2&keywords=jamie+oliver+barbecue

[15] https://www.amazon.co.uk/Barbecue-Bible-10th-Anniversary-ebook/dp/B0075KQ566/ref=sr_1_1?ie=UTF8&qid=1491330986&sr=8-1&keywords=the+barbecue+bible

Keep the food simple... remember hygge doesn't need luxury, so there's no need to go all Waitrose. Shop bought burgers are perfect, unless you really like making them and find it fulfilling. You're aiming to enjoy the company, not to impress anyone.

And keep the numbers down. A hyggely evening is not created by having all the world and his wife over. Choose two or three couples, or just one couple with their family, and concentrate on being close to them. By the end of the evening you should be relaxed with each other, friends, chatting freely. Even if you aren't, try again another week with different friends, because sometimes hygge doesn't happen, even if the situation's perfect. It won't be forced, remember? Either the chemistry is right and you get it or.... Well, cut your losses and enjoy the evening. Nothing ruins hygge quicker than a host who is uptight.

A Hygge Nook member who loves eating in her garden wrote this comment on the group's Facebook page: *"Making outdoor eating a real experience with fresh linen & jars of home grown flowers. Chatting & eating with friends as we move from late afternoon sun to evening lights twinkling in the hedges with the cosy warmth of the fire pit & snuggly, home-made blankets to wrap ourselves in. Bliss"*

Adults in the garden have an advantage that children don't. It's entirely possible that you'll still be there talking as the darkness creeps in and the stars come out. And if that happens, my best advice to you is: grab a blanket and lie on the ground. Just watch the skies and be filled with wonder.

There's a part at the beginning of the revamped Doctor Who when the Doctor is explaining to Rose who he is and he says, "Do you know like we were saying, about the earth revolving? It's like when you're a kid, the first time they tell you that the world is turning and you just can't quite believe it 'cause everything looks like it's standing still. I can feel it...the turn of the earth. The ground beneath our feet is spinning at a thousand miles an hour. The entire planet is hurtling around the sun at sixty-seven thousand miles an hour. And I can feel it. We're falling through space, you and me, clinging to the skin of this tiny little world. And, if we let go..."

Watching stars for any length of time is grounding. We are one small speck in a massive universe of power and heat and wonder. If that doesn't put all our problems in perspective, I don't know what will.

Star gazing is even better if you've read up on some of the stories of the skies. Learn the names and shapes of some of the constellations and their myths. There are some very good websites and books[16] out there that will fill the gaps in your

---

[16] https://www.amazon.co.uk/Stories-Stars-Constellations-Susanna-Hislop-ebook/dp/B00LO1T0I2/ref=sr_1_1?ie=UTF8&qid=1491552570&sr=8-1&keywords=constellation+stories is a beautiful book.

knowledge, while there are star map apps available that will show you the constellations, both visible and invisible.

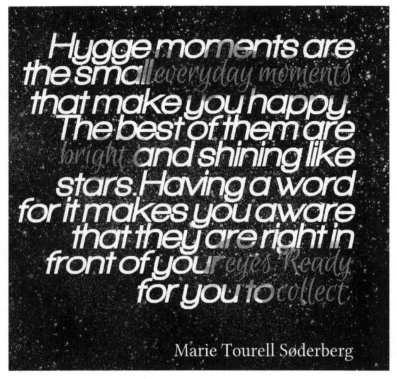

Hygge moments are the small everyday moments that make you happy. The best of them are bright and shining like stars. Having a word for it makes you aware that they are right in front of your eyes. Ready for you to collect.

Marie Tourell Søderberg

At certain times of the year, star gazing can be even more fun due to meteor showers that happen at the same time every year. These vary according to Southern and Northern hemisphere, but you can check on times and dates on Earthsky.org's website[17]. Most famous in the Northern hemisphere are the Perseids, happening mid-August and beautifully timed for late summer watching.

The Best Recipe for Adults in the Garden

[17] http://earthsky.org/astronomy-essentials/earthskys-meteor-shower-guide

Gin and tonic ice lollies, adapted from a recipe on the GinFestival website.[18] Use those cheap plastic moulds that you can buy to make ordinary ice lollies, but be careful and keep these well away from the kids!

Ingredients:

700ml Indian Tonic Water

50ml Gin

12.5ml Fresh Lime Juice

75g Sliced Cucumber

Method:
1. Mix together the gin, tonic and lime juice.
2. Place the cucumber slices into the lolly moulds.
3. Add the gin, tonic and lime juice mix into the mould.
4. Leave overnight to freeze.

It's that easy! And now you have fresh and frosty G&T ice lollies. Of course, if Gin isn't your thing you could always drink cordial with sparkling iced water, or lemonade with crushed strawberries in.

Q: Which is the most hyggely garden?

[18] https://www.ginfestival.com/news/gin-tonic-ice-lollies

A: Of course, the answer is neither... or both. It depends on who is using them and why. The fanciest garden is just a pile of wood, rock and earth if nobody ever uses it, while a small square of yard can be the most hyggely place on earth if the people who gather there love spending time in it alone and with others. That bit about props again, see? The things aren't the hygge... the people are.

Your Garden Hygge homework:

Do you have a garden? If you do, then asking yourself these questions may help you to identify the areas you need to focus on or to improve.

1. Look at your garden. What areas do you know right now are hyggely for you?

2. Who uses the garden? List everybody who usually gets some use out of it during the course of a week. Who uses it most? How?

3. Do you have a seating area? Where is it? What sun or shade does it get? What are the seats like? Does it need anything else to encourage perfect hygge?

4. Do you have a play area? Where is it? What equipment or toys does it have? Who uses it? Does it need anything else to make it a good play area?

5. How do you want to entertain in the garden? Here's a chance to list some people you'd like to invite, or food you want to have a go at making.

6. I know you don't have to buy stuff to achieve hygge, but sometimes things help to create an atmosphere that encourages hygge. Here's your chance to list the things that you have thought of as you read this chapter and that you want to look out for as you go about your business.

Having a hyggely time at the Park

Hanging out for days at a time at the local park can be a great thing to do in the summertime. You don't need children or pets, either. Just take a book and a blanket and make like Belle from Beauty and the Beast. Read, and lose track of the time.

One Hygge Nook member says that one of his favourite ways to hygge in the summer is to sit in the park under a big oak tree with a good book and a cold drink. Most parks have trees of one sort or another.... My local park actually has an oak tree called the Allerton Oak which dates back 1,000 years. Legend has it that the ancient court of Allerton, the Hundred, used to meet under this tree. It's old, gnarled and battered now, a husk of a tree, but you can see how in its prime the branches would have been fantastic cover in the summertime. Perhaps you could choose a tree in your local park that will give you good cover in the hottest of summers. I bet there's stiff competition for it, though!

Get to know your local parks.

Visit them to see what they're like and what facilities they have. Different parks have different personalities, so you may want to keep that in mind as you go around.

So, once you have worked out where your local park is, or which park is best for which activity, what are you going to do there? Well, there are lots of activities available in many parks for free or very little. First step is probably to work out is there a Twitter or Facebook feed for the park and join that. They should send updates and info regularly on events that are planned, or be able to put you in contact with people who use the park for different things. Facilities such as a coffee shop, ice cream shop, a playground area to suit the age of children you have, dog walking area, sports clubs on the field… all these and more may be taking place in the park, so sign up and find out.

Some parks organise their own events, like guided walks or talks about horticulture or history. Often they know things about the park that have passed out of common knowledge. And since many parks are actually the old estates of posh houses of the 19th Century that have been left to the public in perpetuity, the history of the past owners may be really good to know about.

Lack of a decent coffee shop shouldn't stop you turning up to the park: simply bring your own in a thermos flask, pack a basket with cakes or edibles and set off to spend the morning or afternoon running and playing. When it's time for some fika[19], call your group together and sit on a bench or the grass enjoying a restorative pause. My children aren't big tea or coffee drinkers, so I always had a small thermos flask to take with me if I knew there were no facilities at the park.

Of course, the relatively big size of parks makes them ideal for taking a full-blown picnic for lunch. From a plastic bag with the local supermarket's Meal Deal to fold out tables, gazebo and chilled champagne, a picnic can be a wonderful experience. Again, for it to be truly hygge you're not looking at intimidating anyone with the size of your table and spread, and you shouldn't be aiming to get so drunk that you stop anyone else from enjoying themselves, but otherwise anything goes.

I will give you this valuable advice: remember that with a picnic you generally have to carry everything to and from the picnic spot. That means you either have to have a large group all organised to carry heavy hampers, cool boxes and assorted baskets of food, or you should aim to keep it all portable and easily divided between the party.

---

[19] A Swedish word for something sweet and tasty shared at any time in the day. Usually with coffee.

The Bag for Life from the supermarket won't look as pretty as the basket, but it will hold just as much good food, and really with the picnic as with all good hygge meals, it's the food and the company that count.

You don't need to save a picnic at the park for special occasions, either. Taking your sandwiches out to the local green grass area during your lunch break can be just as good. Perhaps you could keep a small fleece blanket or checked tablecloth in your bottom drawer to grab and go at any time.

I love walking around London and seeing the people grabbing a few minutes out on any green space available. Lincoln's Inn Field is always busy, but at lunchtime on a summer's day it's packed with tourists and workers just seeking a break in the sun.

Meeting up with a social group for a bring-and-share experience can be a beautiful thing to do. Choose a day, set up an alternative for if it rains, and pick a meeting spot that everybody can easily find. Everybody makes a variety of food, sits in their friendship groups and voila! A large, friendly picnic with the opportunity of smaller, more hyggely conversation. Which groups do you belong to that could benefit from building fellowship through spending time together? Parents and children at school, Guides, Scouts, the Women's Institute, basically any friendship group could hold a picnic and enjoy the benefits of fresh air, food and fellowship.

When the Sun is shining and the temperature's high, the park may have just the area you need, especially if there's dense planting above and across the paths. Look out for any botanical gardens, or rhododendron walks. These usually grow exceedingly high and dense, thus providing a wonderful level of shade. Even better if there are benches along the way, so you can sit and cool down on the hottest day.

And talking about keeping cool brings me to ice creams. There is nothing more blissful than having a good ice cream on a hot day. And yet, there is nothing more hideous than a bad ice cream that is too sweet and melts too easily.

Ice cream shouldn't be a daily treat, it's much better to be selective and make sure that you have a really good quality one that has a fantastic flavour. We are so lucky in that our local park actually has an ice cream parlour that serves 26 different flavours of ice cream made locally in Cheshire. It's an occasional treat, given the price, but that makes it even more special. If we had one every day or even every time we visited the park then it would just be part of the routine, and routines become boring. As it is, having an ice cream is elevated to a ritual, with the need to decide which flavour, decide which size and then to sit or walk and enjoy the experience.

Even on a strict budget, ice creams in the park can be a treat. Budget supermarkets very often do packs of 6 or 8 choc ices or ice lollies for very little, and keeping them in a padded lunchbag with ice wrap or boxes around them would mean they lasted until you reach the green, green grass of the park. A treat at the park, on a budget.

Entertaining children at the park should be easy:

There's usually a playground, plenty of people to watch and often a place to eat or buy sweets or ice cream from. Yet sometimes even the biggest ice cream loses its thrill, and you can only dash around on the roundabout in the heat for so long. At those times, it helps to have a few ideas up your sleeve that can be done easily and cheaply.

I'm a fan of things that the children can do slightly unsupervised. If they're in a contained area like the park and they know not to run away (we're probably talking 6 or 7 years plus here) then having a small bit of freedom to be 'away from Mum' can be very empowering. I'm not talking completely free to roam, but within limits, say a defined area, or a certain length of time of absence. Going to buy their own sweets or drinks can be a good example. Of course, make sure your child is stranger aware and knows what to do if they don't feel safe.

In our park (yes, I know I keep talking about our park: it's because it's such a good place. Read, consider, adapt or ignore the advice. Your park will be your park and you know what you can do there): like I said *In Our Park* there are several sorts of shut off areas like fields with hedges around, the playground built next to a ha-ha[20] from the original garden landscaping and a hilly area that is called the Rockery but functioned more as an impregnable Mountain to my boys when young. I would let them play there while I sat on the nearby lawn and entertained their younger sister.

I found that having something like a few small plastic ziplock bags to hand meant we could do treasure hunts around the park, especially during the late days of summer. Find a red leaf, can you find a round stone, find a fir-cone. Keep the hunts short, simple and doable, so no asking for gold coins or jewellery.

I'm thinking that treasure hunts lead naturally on to geo-caching when they're older. This involves using a GPS or GPS enabled mobile phone to hunt down and find hidden treasure. Like Pokémon Go, but for real! Look on the geocache website[21] for more information.

With paper and crayons, you can have a bark rubbings hunt. See how many different textures you can find in the park, from triangular to circular to stripes. Using a combination of the natural and man-made it should be possible to collect quite a few. Take the pictures home with you and use them to make

---

[20] Never heard of a ha-ha? Look it up on Wikipedia https://en.wikipedia.org/wiki/Ha-ha and then look out for them at the posh houses you visit.

[21] https://www.geocaching.com/play

summer bunting for the garden, or flowers to stick on the windows.

Check on closing time at your local park. Depending how late it stays open, or how easy it is to access, it may be that summer evenings are an ideal chance to go for walks that are too hot in the heat of the day. Evening walks will probably be cooler, and may be a good chance for the whole family to get some fresh air together after a sticky day at work or school.

Evening opening may also give you a chance to suggest that any groups or clubs you belong to get outside. My daughter used to be a Guide, and during the summer term they moved all their meetings outside, often to the nearby park for den-building or a go at orienteering.

Do check on any park rules or etiquette. Are there any areas that specifically ban dogs, or areas that are set aside for picnics? It's no use setting out a beautiful after school picnic if the field is going to be taken over by football or cricket almost as soon as you've set it out.

Your Park Hygge Homework

1. List all your local parks. Next to each one, write what they're good for e.g. dog walking, play area, miniature train rides.

2. List all the things you want to do in a park

3. Look at the two lists. Can you do everything you want to in one park, or will you need to think about having a few regular parks to visit?

4. Choose a weekend and plan a visit to the park with friends.

5. Planning a holiday? Don't forget to look for any local parks on the tourist website. An afternoon spent in the open air may be just the break you need mid-vacation.

Hygge on the Beach

In Britain, no town is more than 70 miles from a beach (in Denmark, that distance drops to 35 miles!). Whether the beach is one you want to go to, is a different matter. Resorts in Britain range from deserted stretches of sand disturbed only by dog walkers or the occasional Ministry of Defence tank to Blackpool, Brighton and Skegness, where holiday makers have traditionally enjoyed fish and chips in bracing breezy conditions.

My local beach, of course, is Crosby: industrial, often dirty & covered by dogs, it's also famous for the Another Place art installation by Anthony Gormley.

22

Although it's not a beach I'd strip off and swim at, the combination of maritime industrial chic and the striking statues is irresistible. And the beach faces West so there's always a chance of a stunning sunset if you're there at the right time.

So, you're on the beach with the family or some friends. It's summer time, you have some food, probably a seat and you're after some hyggely time. What do you do?

Take Time to Just Be

Firstly, why not try doing nothing at all. At all. Just sit and watch the waves lap the shore, the people walking up and down the beach, the children, the dogs, any swimmers: basically, just sit. Talk to your people. About anything. About everything. Time spent free to do nothing is precious, so indulge.

But after a while (a long while for some of us) even wasting time doing nothing will pall, so you will want to make the most of your time on the beach. What can you do to enjoy your beach time that won't be too hard or require too much stuff?

---

[22] Thanks to Steve Cornforth for the permission to use this photo.

Time you enjoy wasting, was not wasted.

JohnLennon

www.howtohyggethebritishway.com

"Use the Shores, Luke." (Ben Kenobi, Star Wars)

Well, the beach is a brilliant source of natural resources, so have a look around and see what your beach has. I love to walk along the sea strand and collect the small stones and shells that catch my eye.

I really love finding small pieces of sea glass, bits of broken bottles and glass that have been worn to a translucency that makes them irresistible when displayed in a jar besides the window. I can't resist pocketing them and bringing them back home. I love the interplay of manmade object and natural forces at work. It grounds me, and reminds me that however powerful Man becomes, Nature's forces can be just that bit stronger.

Perhaps because there are so many natural features on the beach, it's one of the best places for me to feel at home in nature. I love looking at the natural features and many wonders of the seaside and feeling the force of nature.

Shells tell the stories of the creatures that made them. Collecting different kinds and working out what sort of animal lived within makes for an enjoyable breather in a busy holiday. Either search online or invest in a book to help you recognise the shells. *Spirals in Time*[23] is a beautifully curious book by marine biologist Helen Scales that tells us the story behind the shells: the animals that made them, the history of shells and how humans have made use of them throughout history as currency and decoration. For a more straight-forward guide, *The Photographic Recognition Guide to Seashells of the World* from the Smithsonian has almost every kind of shell you could meet in.

---

[23] https://www.amazon.co.uk/Spirals-Time-Curious-Afterlife-Seashells-ebook/dp/B00SJ90AN6/ref=sr_1_10?ie=UTF8&qid=1491419513&sr=8-10&keywords=book+of+seashells

A book that I was gifted when first I became a mother and that has influenced my visits to the sea ever since is *Gift From the Sea* by Anne Morrow Lindbergh. This small book carries a lot of reassurance and help for women feeling crushed under the responsibilities of life. She talks of taking care of your *self,* of resting rather than doing and of choosing what you keep in your life carefully. To pick one shell each year rather than to fill your pockets greedily. It's over 60 years old, and yet still as readable.

But while you're on the beach, do make the most of the shells. Collect them into piles, make patterns with them, play Tic Tac Toe or decorate your Sandcastle with them. Remember that the whole shells of today become the sand of tomorrow, so enjoy their beauty while you may. **Life is transient.**

Shells featured highly in the advice the members of The Hygge Nook gave me for their summer hygge. One member wrote that "Another thing I loved in my childhood (childhyg?) was going to the beach and collecting shells and looking for the smoothest pebbles. I'll always remember the day my brother and I came home from a morning at the beach with my aunt with a bagful of tiny fish we'd found washed up on the shore... funnily enough my mum wasn't as excited as we were!" I wonder why.

Look at the geology of the beach. Depending on which beach you visit, it may well have a high percentage of rocks. I remember being blasted the first time I walked on Bognor Regis beach and realising that the rocks there were different from the rocks on the beaches I know best in Wales. There were rocks and pebbles in colours and shapes I hadn't seen before, and they weathered differently. I have never seen a rock with a hole in on a North Wales beach: I found several just in one walk along the South Coast beach. I had to bring just a couple of small ones home with me.

Try and work out what sort of rocks you're holding. A good website is The British Geological Society, especially their page on beach pebbles[24]. They explain clearly what sorts of rocks end up on the beach and how they get there. As the first line of the webpage says "Pick up a pebble and hold the story of the Earth in your hand."

And rocks are beautiful to play with. I once spent a glorious afternoon collecting the rocks and pebbles on the beach and making my very own art installation... no more than 10 inches tall!

---

[24]
http://www.bgs.ac.uk/discoveringGeology/geologyOfBritain/holidayguides/pebbles.htm

You can see another beach activity that we had great fun with in the photo above: sand writing. It's fun to write names or words on a stretch of sand that you know is going to be washed away. If you can write it and then climb back up a cliff to watch the sea wash them away, even better!

Almost any activity on the beach can help you to feel hyggely. If you take hygge as an appreciation of the little or simple things in life, then hanging around on a beach has to be one of the simplest pleasures. And finding something to do that can involve everybody is a really hyggely idea.

Our favourite beach in Wales has a cliff behind and natural streams that run off from it to the sea. The water is clear, but I wouldn't drink it. It does run down in little rivulets to the sea making little streams along the beach. Many pleasant afternoons have been spent trying to dam them and make paddling pools only to see the power of the water destroy the small sand banks and keep flowing down to the sea. It's fun to watch the children cooperate and dig harder, deeper, bigger to try and keep the water in one place. A lesson in futility for everyone.

Another great task that involves everybody is building sandcastles. You knew I had to mention it! I would counsel against making the building competitive, which is the quickest way to kill a hyggely feeling, and in favour of getting everybody to build the biggest castle all together than they can.

Working as a team will get a bigger, better castle, while the more engineering-minded amongst your group can plan how to get the moat filled as the sea comes in. Just Google 'impressive sandcastles' to get some intimidatingly good ideas to aim for.

Sand also makes a fantastic art material. Sand sculptures are fantastic to watch being made, but they're also fun to make. Choose a simple shape, like a Sun or a Moon, or an animal that comes from the sea like turtles, dolphins or fish. If you have a good artist in the group, then get them to draw an outline on the sand to make the relief sculpture.

One afternoon, I remember, I made a car facing out to sea, with a footwell and seat large enough for two small bodies to sit in. With a bag of sweets and a bucket and spade, the two littlest children played in it all afternoon.

Not surprisingly, the 'car' took them to the seaside... but the trip to the supermarket was a little less expected, especially when it turned out all the supermarket sold was seaweed!

More human activities are available

Sometimes you need to do more than just bathe in Mother Nature's bounty. It's good to have a few more activities up your sleeve to pull out in the face of boredom.

Know where the local ice cream shop is. In Wales, at both Criccieth and Port Madoc the local ice cream shop is Cadwaladers. They make beautiful ice creams in a range of flavours and are a worthy treat after a day spent rock-pooling or building a castle. Since we usually only visit both these towns once or twice at most on the holiday, the ice cream keeps its Treat status and is an eagerly anticipated moment of pleasure in the day. The fact that both shops are off the beach also gives a natural break to a day spent by the seaside.

Take a ball and play. Take a large ball and play football, or a couple of beach balls and use the ideas on sites such as Babygizmo[25] or the Canadian site Active for Life[26] as inspiration.

I have to put a word of warning in for making sure you're not making a holy mess of noise on a beach that is full of adults quietly appreciating nature, but if you're on a beach full of other families and noisy groups, then go for it.

---

[25] https://babygizmo.com/10-games-you-can-play-with-a-beach-ball/

[26] http://activeforlife.com/21-active-beach-games/

Make the most of whatever the weather throws at you. Sunbathing needs a sunny day, of course, but the rest of the activities on the beach don't need hot and humid, in fact they can actually be even better without the heat of the day. Rock-pooling can be interesting in the rain, since some fish appear who usually hide and, I am reliably informed, crabbing benefits, much like fishing does, from a gentle patter of drizzle. Crabbing is a useful activity to plan for, needing very little more than a bit of bacon bait, a paperclip and a strong length of fisherman's line. It also takes a little patience and the right place to fish from. Some beaches may have jetties or a short pier to throw the line off, since crabs prefer to shelter in the dark under the jetty for most of the day. Look for a deeper rockpool and keep a bucket nearby to keep the crabs in. Handy tips on crabbing can be found on the Countryfile website[27].

Rockpooling, relying as it does on balance and a willingness to step on the wet and squelchy side of nature, was never one of my children's favourite activities.

We did go looking at the pools, and sometimes stood still long enough to see the fantastic fauna that lives in these little ecosystems, but my children aren't natural fishermen, so they soon went off to explore elsewhere. Hygge is different for everyone, see?

---

[27] http://www.countryfile.com/explore-countryside/food-and-farming/how-go-crabbing-kids

Take along something to do. I'm never knowingly without a craft project on the go at any one time, usually a crochet blanket of one kind or another, but even I find a blanket isn't the right project to take to the beach. I love finding small fiddlings to do, like flowers, hearts or amigurumi toys, that take minutes to make and can wait for their stuffing. Finding a small, portable craft to do is a good solution for people like me who find their hands get impatient without something to mess with.

Whatever I take to the beach, I try and keep away from anything requiring batteries. Although I am a Kindle girl through and through, my beach reads will be paper, a magazine or a cheap book that I don't mind getting wet. I do take the phone, for emergency calls and to use as a camera if I want one, but many of my times on the beach pass unnoticed and unrecorded. It's better that way: I know that they were days when I had nothing else to do except be present and enjoy life

Eating on the beach can be heaven or hell, depending on the attitude you take towards it. Happy memories of tomato sandwiches with sand adding a certain *je ne sais quoi* or of the part-raw, part-burned sausages of an impromptu beach barbecue could be either. Let's give them the gloss of nostalgia and say that if you are going to spend any time on the beach, food will be a part of that experience at some time, so you might as well accept that either you need to pack a full tarpaulin with table and vacuum cleaner to suck up all the sand there will be, or you accept that eating on the beach will not be free from sand. Put yourself in the right frame of mind, and approach it as an adventure.

I love this advice from one Hygge Nook member, "I love having an impromptu picnic on the beach to watch the sun go down, coming home from work and packing a picnic and a few beers for an impromptu tea on the beach to watch the sun go down with my fiancé." Romantic, or what?

Of course, the food doesn't have to be on the beach. A different Hygge Nook member wrote that she loved "A long stroll along an almost deserted beach, hearing the sea birds screaming and the waves rattling the shingle. Searching that shingle for sea glass, fossils and pretty pebbles. Ending up in a pretty, friendly café for a cream tea and chat. Perfect." Sounds perfect to me as well.

There is pleasure in the pathless woods, there is rapture in the lonely shore, there is society where none intrudes, by the deep sea, and music in its roar; I love not Man the less, but Nature more.

LordByron

www.howtohyggethebritishway.com

My husband thinks that the seaside is the invention of the Devil. He doesn't like sand or water and the holidays we've taken have been a sort of torture to him in so many ways. Once we invested in a couple of beach chairs, the easily fold downable ones, he was happier. He still thinks eating on the beach is unhygienic and he hates sand near any of his food.

For him, the best time to eat on a day at the beach is before you go down onto the sands and after you come off. I have tried, but he won't play Pollyanna about the beach. Because hygge is about making sure that everyone feels relaxed, I try to ensure that we eat on the beach sometimes to give me my hyggely moment, and that at other times we save food for the walk along the sea front.

I have to agree with one of the members of the Hygge Nook who said that beach-time hygge for her was "strolling along the beach with my family and the dog then sitting with chips and watching the waves roll up on the to the beach."

Fish and chips eaten near to the sea must be as close to perfect match of place and food as you can get. There are certainly advantages to finding a decent Fish'n'chips restaurant in a small seaside town and having a fish supper when you've spent the day on the beach. My husband (again) doesn't like to eat al fresco, so his idea of heaven would be a proper fish supper eaten in the fish restaurant, minus any mushy peas but with battered plaice, chips and sliced buttered bread. With a pot of tea and a promenade stroll to follow, it's the height of elegance.

I was raised a lot less refined. I'm happy to eat my fish and salted chips from the paper with a wooden fork. Sitting looking out at the waves, tired after a day of nothingness except bathing in nature's beauty and ready for sleep in a short while, I remember eating fish and chips as a family on our annual beach holiday and enjoying the taste of the hot fish while a cool breeze swept over the Bristol channel. Both ways of eating are hygge, if the company is right and you feel happy.

Stretch out the days on the beach into night times. If you are there with a large enough group of friends, then finding a way to spend some part of the evening on or near the beach can be very hyggely. Evening walks along the prom, a moonlit paddle on the seastrand, or a beach picnic sat at the end of the jetty can all extend the time available at the beach. Some beaches run organised events at night time, others are simply open for you to use.

One glorious summer evening in the early eighties, the Concert Band I belonged to organised a beach party in Ainsdale, a particularly lovely stretch of coast near to us. We arrived in the late afternoon, and played cricket, volleyball and other games on the sand before moving to the shelter of the dunes. We had a campfire, toasted sausages and marshmallows in it, ate foil wrapped bananas and chocolate, sat around, drank (alcohol or soft drinks according to age) and, since we were a musical bunch, ended up with singing and dancing to the guitar that one member had brought along. As I think about it now, I can still feel the love and togetherness we felt. That must be nearly 40 years ago now, but the hyggely feeling that memory gives never goes.

Check up on the rules about staying on the beach. Because they can be so long and deserted, there can be local issues with gangs and noise. Fires may not be allowed, especially if there's a risk of setting dune grass alight, but barbecues may be. Use your common sense and if you do light a fire keep it small, easily controlled and make sure you extinguish it well when you leave.

And it goes without saying, take your rubbish away.

The hardest skill to develop by the seaside is the patience to wait for the gift from the sea. So much anticipation and anxiety can be tied up with a trip to the seaside, especially if you only go once or twice a year, because you want it to be right. You want the perfect seaside time, the ideal sunset, the crispest fish and softest chips, the fish to nibble your toes, the right sea-glass to fall into your hand.

Relax. The seaside is a natural force. You won't get what you want from it by looking. There's a fair amount of letting go of expectations needed to get the most from the sea. Stop searching for the ideal, the best, the one. Take what you're given and be grateful. It rains? So what, put your mac on and laugh through it. You fall over and scrape your leg? Bathe it in clean water, slap on a plaster and smile at the thought of a scar that will remind you forever of a day by the sea.

Just wait… and the gift of the sea will come to you. Not always something you can lift up or fit in a pocket, but perhaps a sea glass nugget of memory that you will take out and look at in later times. A feeling of peace and togetherness… pure hygge… the scent memory of salt and seaweed and sweet candyfloss or a smile that grows when you hear a seagull pass by. And peace… always peace. The sea is a wild thing, that can never be tamed.

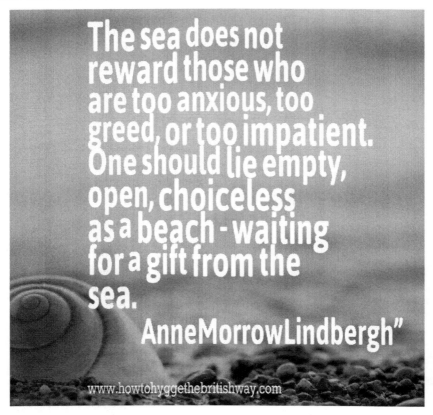

The sea does not reward those who are too anxious, too greed, or too impatient. One should lie empty, open, choiceless as a beach - waiting for a gift from the sea. AnneMorrowLindbergh"

www.howtohyggethebritishway.com

Your Beach Hygge homework:

Have you ever just sat at the beach and listened? It can be a tremendously grounding activity. Just sit and watch the clouds, the waves, the birds. If you have, close your eyes now and think back to the sounds and sensations you remember.

1. What parts of being by the seaside do you remember most? Why?

2. Do you know where your nearest or favourite beach is? How often do you get there? Can you plan a trip there this year?

3. Jot down any activities you think you want to do at the beach this year. Make a note of any special resources you'd need for them.

4. If you can't get to a beach, can you plan a beach party at home? Download some meditation music that features the sounds of the sea, or make up a playlist of your favourite beach music (the Beach Boys, Don Henley, party hits you love) and act as if you're by the beach. Put up a windbreak, lay out the towels, get a bucket of sand to sprinkle around and about. Play beach, or as I like to say "Fake it til you make it"!

Finding Hygge in the Wild

Getting out into the wild is good for you. There's proven scientific evidence[28] that spending time outside in green spaces reduces stress, lowers blood pressure and improves short term memory. It's even likely that spending increasing amounts of time in the proper wild will lengthen your life. Scandinavian countries have a long history of encouraging time in the wild, with Friluftsliv, or free air living in Norway and Sweden being a much-encouraged practice. Some even credit it for part of the reasons why the Nordic nations score so highly in Happiness charts.

Little wonder, then, that there is increasing concern about the lack of 'wild-time' children are getting. A 2016 article from The Guardian newspaper[29] stated that "A fifth of the children (surveyed) did not play outside at all on an average day", while a massive 75% of the children surveyed spent less time outside than a prison inmate who, by law, gets one hour of exercise outside a day.

---

[28] http://uk.businessinsider.com/scientific-benefits-of-nature-outdoors-2016-4?r=US&IR=T/#10-improved-mental-health-10

[29] https://www.theguardian.com/environment/2016/mar/25/three-quarters-of-uk-children-spend-less-time-outdoors-than-prison-inmates-survey

You should sit in nature for 20 minutes a day... Unless you're busy, then you should sit for an hour.

Old Zen Proverb

www.howtohyggethebritishway.com

Even a trip to the local park or small wood can help, but if you want the total wild experience, you may need to look further afield.

Now, I'm not talking about actual wildernesses here, at least, not in Britain. So much of our land is either lived on or worked that to get actual wildness in England is difficult, certainly if you're thinking in terms of vast stretches of uninhabited territory. You need to go to Canada or Alaska for that. In the UK the best chance of landscape approaching a wilderness is the Highlands of Scotland and some parts of the mountainous regions of England and Wales.

I think we don't need to go too wild to feel wild here. Let's define 'wild' for ourselves.

A wild area is one that

    a. Shows no obvious sign of habitation

    b. Has a lively ecosystem with a good level of diversity of animal and plant life

    c. Doesn't have running water, flushing toilets and an electricity point fitted as standard

That expands the amount of 'wild' areas available to us quite a bit, doesn't it?

Making hygge in the wild can be as simple or as complicated as you want it to be. Basically you have to work out which is the best way to access the countryside for you.

1. Make do with the suburban or inner city greens and wild areas that are available.

2. Have day trips into the surrounding wild areas of the countryside, by any form of transport.

3. Stay in the countryside and enjoy the experience of it at night as well.

Urban Wilderness.

There is a lot to be said for making use of any green or open space near you. Not everybody has access to miles of rolling countryside, but most towns and cities have areas that could be called 'wild' or at the very least are proper 'countryside'. It is actually interesting how quickly you pass from conurbation to countryside in some parts of the country. I have to put a massive shout out for Newcastle Upon Tyne here, where a simple journey of 15 minutes North will get you into vast stretches of open countryside and, further along, the forest of Kielder. I know vast amounts of the countryside are farmed, and not wild, but time spent in any green and pleasant land is good.

Look on the websites for your local towns or cities to see if there are any areas that you aren't aware of. I will never forget my surprise on learning that what I thought of as a small wood a bare 150 yards from my house actually gave way to vast fields of wildlife that could have been anywhere, such was the peace. It's a regular walk now. There is just something so peaceful about walking through deep grass and getting off the paths that appeals to me. And there's excellent blackberry picking to be done in August and September.

You're looking for uncultivated areas, not municipal park. Look for wildlife reserves or areas that promote themselves as good for wildlife diversity. They're the sort of places where you will see the butterflies, hear the birds and watch the small

mammals that are usually driven out by neat borders and tarmac paths. The Countryfile Magazine website listed 18 of the best in the UK in an article[30], pointing out the hidden gems such as St Nicholas Fields in York, Camley Street Natural Park in London and Sunnybank Nature Reserve in Sheffield which it describes as 'lurking behind a petrol station'.

Despite cuts in funding, many volunteers often help to raise funds for wildlife trusts or to lay on events to teach the next generation about the animals that often share our habitat. Look up online, or ask around your group for advice on what areas are close to you.

---

[30] http://www.countryfile.com/countryside/18-britains-urban-wildlife-havens

And make the most of Nature's bounty in the city. Hygge Nook members were quick to extol the virtue of using free produce. They recommended collecting elderflowers early in the summer and making elderflower cordial from them. It takes less than 30 minutes to prepare.

Elderflower Cordial

1. *Gently rinse over 30 elderflower heads to remove any dirt or little creatures.*

2. *Pour 3 pints of boiling water over 2lbs sugar in a very large mixing bowl. Stir well and leave to cool.*

3. *Add 2oz citric acid, slices from 2 oranges and 3*

4. *lemons, and then the flowers.*

5. *Leave in a cool place for 24 hours, stirring occasionally.*

6. *Strain through some muslin and transfer to sterilised bottles.*

I'm not sure where the best place for elderflowers is, but a search online should help you to find and recognise them. I find it safer to stick with blackberries, which come in from early August onwards. Picking them and then cooking them to make pies is an afternoon's work, but eating the pie in the end is a great reward.

Hygge is about an appreciation of the simple things in life: learning to appreciate the wonders of nature that can bloom and survive despite the best attempts of man is simple, but a gift that will last a lifetime.

We need the tonic of wildness...At the same time that we are earnest to explore and learn all things, we require that all things be mysterious and unexplorable, that land and sea be indefinitely wild, unsurveyed and unfathomed by us because unfathomable. We can never have enough of nature.

HenryDavidThoreau

www.howtohyggethebritishway.com

Being a Daytripper

With the growth of train and car transport from the early 20th century onwards, places that had been inaccessible due to the time required to get to them suddenly became within reach of a short drive or a train ride to the nearest station. And with the Holiday Pay Act of 1938 guaranteeing all workers paid holidays, on top of the Bank Holidays Act in 1871, suddenly workers actually had free time and access to a world beyond their horizons.

I live in Liverpool, a beautiful place and the fourth most visited city by overseas visitors. The great advantage of Liverpool is that, within a drive of less than 2 or 3 hours, you can be in Snowdonia in Wales, in the Lake District, in the Peak District of Derbyshire, the North Yorkshire Moors, The Dales of West Yorkshire, the scenery of Wenlock Edge in Shropshire. All close enough to visit just for a day, all stunning scenery and all excellent places to walk and admire nature. I am truly fortunate to live here.

Making the most hygge out of a day trip requires the same use of common sense and (with children) often the same degree of planning and coordination as a longer vacation does. Any time you are proposing to walk in the mountains or hills of the UK you should be very aware of the weather and be aware that it can change at a moment's notice.

Read up on the district you are visiting, plan what equipment you need to carry with you and make sure that you plot your route just enough that someone knows roughly where you should be just in case.

Investing in good quality equipment that spreads the load, decent waterproof shoes and good socks are practical considerations you need to have in place as well. If your physical comfort is taken care of, and your Mother's mental well-being alleviated by knowing roughly where you'll be, then the rest of the time is your own to hygge with whomever you wish.

I love walking in a small group of friends. Some of the best conversations I've had have happened when walking along a mountain path.

There is just something about the view that encourages deep thinking, a consciousness of our place in the world and a thankfulness for those who are sharing the journey (metaphorically and actually) with us.

Using public footpaths requires you to know where they are. The best bet here is to buy the Ordnance Survey map of the area and to use it to plot the walk, unless you have got the details of the walk from a place you trust to have them correct. I found having the map was still a good thing for me, as I love map-reading and finding the features I could see on the map in real life.

You have a moral duty to take care of the countryside, especially where you may be crossing private land. Be aware of gates, animals and machinery and be sure to follow the Countryside Code[31].

---

[31] Most of the Code is common sense: respect animals and property, take nothing but photographs, leave nothing but footprints. You can find the full code here: https://www.gov.uk/government/publications/the-countryside-code

Obviously, leave no rubbish, take nothing but pictures. Copies of the Countryside Code are available to download from the UK government website. Drawn up by the government of the UK in the 1930s when greater mobility meant that town dwellers were getting back to the countryside in greater numbers than ever before, while traffic was beginning to show its true potential for trouble, the code can be summed up in three memorable words: respect, protect and enjoy.

Experiencing the Countryside at Night

Although walking or travelling through the areas, then retreating to a warm bed can be very hyggely, spending time out in the forests or fields of the countryside and then sleeping nearby in a tent or pod can give a greater feeling of being part of the wild, in which case you have the choice of using authorised campsites or an idea growing in popularity as a way of experiencing the full wilderness, Wild Camping.

Here I put my hands up and confess that the only camping I've ever done was as a Cub Scout Leader in an organised Scout camping area, so I am not the best person to ask for advice on camping and enjoying the open air under canvas. I have to rely upon the advice of my camping friends.

Wild camping without the landowner's permission is actually illegal in parts of Britain, and certainly your tent can be removed if you are trespassing. It is, however, growing in popularity. The best advice I've read is arrive late, leave early and leave no mess. There are some good websites out there to give advice on wild camping, and Michelle McGagh in her book, *The No-Spend Year: How You Can Spend Less and Live More*[32] has an excellent chapter on a week's wild camping holiday she had.

3232   https://www.amazon.co.uk/No-Spend-Year-spend-less-ebook/dp/B01LXW6CJR/ref=sr_1_1?ie=UTF8&qid=1495020725&sr=8-

A word has to be put in here to remind you that if you do go wild camping, being mindful of the environment and other people takes priority over having a wild time. Wild camping has actually been banned in the Loch Lomond National Park due to anti-social behaviour and alcohol. The rules set out by Alan Rogers on his Wild Camping website[33] are excellent advice for anyone setting out into the countryside, even if only for a day trip.

"As more campers find themselves in the wilderness, the 'leave no trace' motto has become ever important to preserve and protect these vital areas.

There are seven key principles to familiarise yourself with and adopt on your next wild camping experience.

*1. **Plan Ahead and Prepare:** Preparation should be a key component of any trip, but particularly when camping. Use a map and familiarise yourself with the area, find out if there are any specific rules for hikers and campers, and only travel in small groups.*

*2. **Avoid disrupting the land:** It's advised to camp only on durable lands, which would mean trails and campsites. Try to avoid creating a new path or campsite, which would disrupt the purity of the land.*

*3. **Properly dispose of waste:** Take home everything you bring away with you, including all rubbish. You should also bury human waste properly, in a hole* *between 6 and 8 inches deep and 50 metres from water.*

*4. **Leave what you find:** You should leave everything you find onsite, including rocks and plants. No matter how attractive you find it or how well it'd go in your living room, leave it behind!*

*5. **No campfires:** You should never light an exposed fire when camping in the wild. Instead, use specialist stoves to cook your food.*

*6. **Respect the wildlife:** Leave all wildlife alone. This not only protects the environment but also ensures your safety. Don't leave food around for animals and never feed them.*

*7. **Consider others:** Respect fellow campers and hikers by not creating too much noise, and by yielding to them on a trail. Let everyone else enjoy the environment as you are."*

Worth learning by heart, and living by, I think.

Open your eyes, look up to the sky and see....

If you are in the wilderness... or what passes for it in the UK... then make the most of it. Go back and read the bit on stargazing in Hygge in the Garden, because hopefully the light pollution in the middle of the countryside will be far less than in a town or city. There should be stars beyond counting above your head, and all the stars in various constellations that are usually little winks will be bright blinking dots.

I have been told, but never seen for myself, that if you are in a dark enough place you can see the Milky Way[34], like a spilled glass of milk, spreading across the sky. That's our galaxy, a mass of between 100 and 400 billion stars, circling slower than life and faster than light. 100 billion possible planets circling the stars and the light from the furthest point that we see has taken 112,900,000,000 years to reach Earth. If that doesn't put our puny lives into perspective, nothing will.

There are designated Dark Sky Parks across the world. These are areas that promise to keep as free from light pollution as possible so that the sky is dark enough to see many more stars than usual.

---

[34] https://en.wikipedia.org/wiki/Milky_Way

In the UK, five areas have been accredited with Dark Sky Park status: The Cairngorms, The Brecon Beacons, Exmoor in Devon, The Lake District and parts of Northumberland including around Kielder. If you're ever lucky enough to stay at any of these, make the most of it. The Dark Sky Discovery[35] site has plenty of good advice on finding and using dark sky spaces near you.

The miracle of man is not how far he has sunk but how magnificently he has risen. We are known among the stars by our poems, not our corpses.

Robert Ardrey

www.howtohyggethebritishway.com

Your Wild Hygge Homework:

1. Write a list of all the wild places you can think of near you. It could be woods, trails, urban wildlife reserves, country parks, anything that can be you mixing with nature.

2. What do you need to encourage you to go wild? Do you need to borrow or buy anything? Keep a list here of things you'd like to have the use of for a camping or walking expedition.

3. Make a date and stick to it. Go for that walk you've always fancied. Get out to the parkland you know exists a short drive away. Go and find a friend to visit a dark park with. It's easy to make a plan, much harder to execute it. Make a promise to yourself that getting out into nature will be something you do for yourself and your health as a gift.

Zoo Hygge

Zoos are hygge? Yes, because animals are hygge. With a very few exceptions, most animals have got the 'sit around and be happy with life' role off pat. We can learn much from spending some time watching a lion or jaguar enjoy their life, or from watching an otter glide elegantly through the water.

Animals teach us much about enjoyment as well. Watch a sealion swimming and jumping in their pool and you can't help but smile. Similarly with penguins. When they're earthbound they are inelegant, funny walkers with funny beaks. Watch them slide into the water and see them swimming, and they're magnificent movers, sharp, fast and with a turn that would make a London Taxi blush.

Your first question, then, is safari park or zoo?

The answer to that is that both have their purpose and both give a different experience.

Zoos have their animals more contained, in cages while you walk around. This means you will probably be able to see more animals in a small area and a smaller space, but it does mean you're watching an animal not in its natural environment, confined not free. Some zoos have been accused of making animals feel bored, or not giving each the correct space. Choose your zoo carefully, and don't be afraid to complain if you think the conditions aren't satisfactory.

My nearest zoo is Chester, and I think they do a pretty good job of taking care of the animals. They are always trying to make the enclosures bigger, add interest to the spaces according to what each animal needs. I know they build in puzzles and treasure hunts for food for animals like monkeys and apes that need stimulation.

Safari parks are more open spaces, with you confined in the car or vehicle while the animals wander around you (hopefully). That makes for a closer experience, especially when a lioness just casually walks past your stationary car and takes a bite at the bumper as happened to us one day…

Safari parks can be hot, though, in the middle of summer, and the safari drive is usually designed to be a certain length so you are tied into the full 40 minutes to an hour. You will need to decide which is right for you.

We are lucky enough to have both on the doorstep, so to speak, with Knowsley Safari Park a 10 minute ride away and Chester Zoo a 40 minute drive.

I appreciate that fortune, and the fact that when the children were young we had annual membership at either one or the other meant we spent a lot of time there.

Wild animals are less wild and more human than many humans of this world

MuniaKhan

www.howtohyggethebritishway.com

Annual membership can be well worth it if you live nearby. I was given my first membership at the zoo as a gift when my eldest was a baby. Yes, the drive was 40 minutes there and back again, but I think I took him about once a month until he was two, when I was pregnant again and the whole, brave-days-out thing took a back seat.

With three small children under 5 a few years later, membership of the Safari Park became a real boon. The fact it was only 10 minutes away meant we could go as often as we liked and we weren't waiting for a fine day to go and join the crowds. We never visited on Bank Holidays or at the weekend in the height of summer. You see a completely different side of the animals when you go on a cold, wet February Sunday afternoon, simply because there was nothing on TV and you needed a break. The lions look a lot more fed up, the monkeys huddle for warmth (and climb on far more car bonnets just for the heat of the engine) while a wet, bedraggled otter is just happy it's wet.

Knowing you can go just for a short while and come back again later means you don't feel you have to do everything every time. That's a great facility, because it means you can choose different things to concentrate on each time. Once or twice we visited the Safari Park and bypassed the drive through completely to concentrate on the sealions enclosure, or to visit the birds of prey. We even went once just for the cafeteria and the presence of animals in the park was just an added bonus.

I believe that if children fall in love with wildlife they will grow up wanting to protect it.

ImogenTaylor

www.howtohyggethebritishway.com

What do you do in the zoo?

Well, just watching the animals is a start. Everybody probably has their own favourite animal. My second son was fascinated by rhinos from an early age.

We could spend hours just pulled over in the safari park, or stood by the enclosure in the zoo just watching these giant beasts with their horns and massive feet. I should point out here that Son Number 2 was the smallest and lightest of my three children for most of his growth years. I found it fascinating that he should pick such a symbol of strength and power as his favourite animal.

I love ambling around the zoo or park and stopping wherever my interest falls. Now my children are old enough not to need full-time watching I'm free to stop and stare all I like without being pulled to move on. This means I also get a chance to properly watch an animal. I love watching how the hierarchy of a pack works, or how sealions set each other off on wild chases, how monkeys react to each other, and how meerkats need support from each other to stay alive.

Take your camera or a sketchbook and set out to record a particular animal. Stop at their enclosure, set up a seat or lean against the wall and watch how they move, how they talk to each other. How fast are they, how long do they keep still, do they watch everything or are they focused solely on their food when they eat. Take plenty of pictures, or draw them again and again. You're not concerned about the end product, this is all about the process. The skill of looking closely, of observing and noticing the small details, is a great gift to have. And to lose oneself in concentration, to be in the flow of the moment, that must be good hygge, yes?

Joy in looking and comprehending is nature's most beautiful gift.

AlbertEinstein

www.howtohyggethebritishway.com

Step away from the social media for the duration of the visit. Ban the phones (because all good hygge happens when the phones are in the pocket) and talk with your companions. Build a memory, not a timeline and relive the moment later in a journal entry or a blog post.

Or, contrariwise, do as I did on the last duet visit I made to the Safari Park with my daughter (the summer before she started school full time and the day before her brothers broke up). We went to the Park precisely to record every minute, from her sitting up front in the car, to putting her head out to watch the wallabies.

We had the camera out all the time and took so many photographs. We taped video of our lunch and went to the shop, where we each got a Siberian tiger cub. I knew the chances of a day like this happening again were slim. I set out to enjoy every second of it and after our return we sat and made a storybook, fitting the photos in and writing a story about Sarah's Day at the Park. I still have it on file somewhere.

Take your picnic with you. Food can be expensive at any place you go to during the summer. Packing a picnic and eating it in the car or on any available grass is a good cost saving measure, as well as giving you the opportunity to share a hyggely moment. All good hygge involves food, doesn't it? Some zoos have picnic huts, so even on a wet day you can eat outside. Otherwise, a bench or space on a lawn is good enough for most days.

Never feed or torment the animals, though. Zookeepers spend hours working out a balanced diet, and even though that chimpanzee may be begging you for food, he really shouldn't be fed. Not even your banana.

Look into activities that the zoo or park may provide. Education can be hygge, too! At Chester Zoo they often had art or craft activities that were available for a small fee, or free sometimes, and they provided a few minutes respite on a warm day. There may be zoo tours, or organised displays at feeding time that are worth going to.

At one stage I could almost repeat verbatim the Sealion Show at Knowsley Safari Park myself, we went every time. It was educational, however. I can still tell you the difference between a sealion and a seal, and I know how high a fully grown male sealion can jump to hit a ball.

The shows are great fun for children and adults, and anything that makes you laugh together is hyggely.

Choose a spirit animal from the zoo and keep visiting them. This is tremendously well worth it if you have a year-long pass. Pick a creature that 'speaks' to you, that you feel drawn to or that has characteristics you either have, admire or would like yourself. That's your spirit animal, see? Then watch the group of that animal closely and see if you can choose just one of them. It could be a meerkat with a pink ear, a lioness with a scar on her head, a monkey with black patches over their eyes or some animal that you think you might recognise again. They will be your totem for the year, your symbol of what you want to be.

Watch them for as long as you can, take the pictures or draw them. Point them out to your family, and get them to choose their own. Then, the next time you go, go back and visit them again. Enjoy the experience of watching the same animal every time you go and getting to know them so well that you can say whether on a cold day they'll be inside or out, or whether they eat all the time or just occasionally.

It's not real bonding, but it is putting your interest in something outside of yourself and that can be a valuable lesson. You may want to adopt an animal if the zoo offers that scheme, or donate in their name to an animal charity. Part of feeling at one with the world is bonding with nature, and anything that strengthens that bond is good.

Zoos aren't just for children.

Sometimes it's very easy to think of a place as 'just for kids' and never visit as an adult or with your adult friends, but it's really good fun to give yourself permission to go to places like these with adult friends. It's good to walk and talk, and the zoo provides a wonderful backdrop for interesting discussions that wouldn't happen if you just met up for coffee.

Allow plenty of time for your visit, plan in the refreshments and make a full day/night of it. You can plan a visit before a meal, or have a relaxed lunch at a local pub restaurant and then visit.

If it's a zoo you're familiar with from childhood, enjoy sharing stories of your past. Wandering around gives plenty of opportunity for talking and finding out things about your friends you might never have thought.

That great big man who laughs his way through life? Who'd have thought he was scared of the dark and wouldn't enter the Batcave? The small woman who wouldn't say boo to a goose? Her favourite creature is the scorpion in the insect house. Vicious and toxic: who knew?

Zoo visits as adults can be part nostalgia, part entertainment and part education. We never stop learning, and a trip to a zoo with the express intention of studying one type of animal and finding out as much as possible can be a really valuable experience. How much do you know about camelids, for example? Where do they live? What breeds count as camelids? How do you behave around them? Sometimes I think we box learning off as something we do when we're at school or young, and forget that as adults we need to stretch our brains. It's easy to think of adult education as tied to a classroom, or to day courses from work. Why not inject fun into our learning with a day trip or two as well? Challenge your friend to find out 5 facts while you find five facts, and together you'll have learned 10 things.

If you're feeling wealthy, then you could sign up for a day as a zookeeper and work for your hygge. Sign up for a rhino experience[36] or an elephant experience with your friend and have a unique day out together. You may never want to be a zookeeper for real at the end of it, but I guarantee you'll have learned something about your friendship.

---

36   http://www.chesterzoo.org/support-us/gifts-and-experiences/experience-days/rhino-encounter

We're all working together; that's the secret.

Sam Walton

www.howtohyggethebritishway.com

Your Zoo Hygge Homework:

1. Trips to the zoo can be expensive. Start a zoo fund savings jar, and put your change in it when you come in from the shops. A few pounds a week for a year will cover the cost of entry and, if you're frugal enough, also pay for your picnic as well!

2. Keep a list of zoos you fancy visiting on the page here or in your diary or notebook (I use Evernote online notebook for things like this: I never lose the notes that way)

3. Choose a spirit animal for a year. Even if you can't make it to the zoo, you can still watch animals on documentaries or videos online. Recognising why that animal appeals to you can be a revealing test. I love foxes, because they're quick and clever, owls because they signify wisdom and red pandas because they are cute and cuddly to look at, but dangerous if you get too close. Yes, I know. Very revealing.

4. Even though this is a book on summer hygge, I have to put a plea in here for visiting the zoo in the wintertime as well. It's quieter, there are less people in the way so you can watch the more popular animals for longer, and some animals behave in a completely different way according to the weather. We had a family tradition for a few years of going to the zoo on Boxing Day whatever the weather. Even if it snowed. It was cold, yes… but the hygge of coming inside to drink hot tomato soup and a sausage roll made every bit of ice worth while.

Pack your Hygge with the Toothbrush, it's Holiday Time

What's your holiday style? Beach or city? Country or town? At home or abroad? We all have different holiday preferences and requirements, but one thing we can all include in our holiday plans is hygge.

Hygge Holiday Accommodation.

The first question I'd ask is: **Hotel or Self Catering**? I know different people have different needs, but I'd question whether a hotel can ever really be totally hygge. Someone else decides when you get up, what breakfasts are available and to an extent how you spend your days since, unless the hotel has a lounge bar area, you're doomed to spend the evenings out of the hotel altogether or in your room.

We once tried a hotel break with a baby. Never again. We couldn't go to our room unless the baby was asleep, and then only to sleep ourselves, we tried putting the baby to sleep and going to the hotel restaurant for a meal with the baby monitor only to find…

Surprise, surprise… that Baby woke up and wanted to come too. He was very cute, but it was a long way away from the Anniversary dinner *a deux* we had planned. Our holidays since then have very much been self-catering, thank you, with a kitchen and a living room that we can use at a time that suits us.

Self-catering also allows you to think of a place as home for the length of your stay. That means you don't need to worry about moving things about to suit you. At one cottage, we moved the dining table out into the large lounge from the small kitchen so that there was more space to sit and eat. Of course, we moved it back at the end, rather than leave the place in a mess.

We regularly move beds to suit as well. Camp beds in one room move to another, or it becomes clear that the double room described isn't big enough really and a child ends up on the floor somewhere else... It's your home for the week or fortnight, use it how it suits you.

I would never be afraid to make sure that the house is child-proofed to the age of children you have. It's easy to remember with toddlers: just put everything away. With older children, you may want to put any knick-knacks that are scattered around away, or to move the flower vase off the coffee table to a shelf nearby. Rough play can make a mockery of a beautiful arrangement.

I'd also argue for putting out things that matter to you. If you're a hygge fiend who needs candles, then take some and put them along the mantelpiece or a shelf. Put out a fruit bowl to make holiday snacking healthy (healthier). Put your books and magazines out, line the DVDs up, get the toy box in the corner. This is your space for the duration and it needs to suit you.

I'm not saying you need to go as far as one writer about interiors who put away a flowery bedspread for a one night stay in a hotel because the pattern ruined her scandi-chic aesthetic, but you can always put aside too many covers or cushions. If you have a favourite throw that you bring (especially with children, having a blanket they love with you on holiday is useful) then put it out. Just remember to restore the house to normality at the end.

Here I must extol the virtue of the caravan.

My husband baulks at the mention of caravanning, but I was raised on it as a cheap family holiday and (I have to say) I think it can be very hyggely. It is your very own home from home. You carefully choose the items that furnish it, from cushions to curtains to comfy covers.

It can hold games and toys that your children have chosen, it has the very real play value of being a small house on wheels and, ultimately, the whole allure of being on an adventure like Five Go Off in a Caravan. Even the tasks that surround a caravan holiday, like getting water, doing the washing and getting washed yourself can be hyggely depending on how you approach them. Not emptying the chemical toilet, though. I don't know any way of making that hyggely.

And caravanning also forces you to sit outside. Because the van is too small usually to spend great long chunks of time in, the awning or outdoor seating space gets a lot of use. Children on a caravanning holiday go pretty much free range, as long as the site allows it. (Do check the rules of the site. Some are designed more for the elderly than families)

Some of my Hygge Nook members also love the idea of caravanning, with one member writing that she loves *"caravanning in the UK, sitting down to a full English breakfast with the kids, in the awning or van just watching the world knowing that the day is our own. We have a different garden every weekend!"*

Caravanning suits the younger family or the older couple. It's probably not that good for a city break for a couple. Then it's worth investing in a good hotel. We (my husband and I) love to get away from the children (and now guinea pigs) for a break, and we have found that hotels work well for just the two of us.

Book into a convenient city centre hotel for a City Break.

You can still make the place more hyggely: use a candle, unpack your clothes for anything longer than a night and keep the place looking tidy. Or look for an alternative source of accommodation. Home swap, stay with a friend or a friend of a friend, or rent through a site that lets you use rooms in other people's houses. I haven't used AirBnB[37] myself, but I understand that can be very hyggely, with a house to call your own and sometimes an amenable host to talk to as well.

[37] https://www.airbnb.co.uk/

There is a very real temptation on a city or sight-seeing holiday to plan it thoroughly, to compile lists of places to go and sights to visit. You can, on a week-long holiday, have more places to visit than you have days. Then you spend your days rushing between the places, making sure you've seen everything that there is to see and that everybody has been educated or not to the fullest extent. That's not hyggely.

Better by far to adopt a relaxed attitude to sight-seeing and view the holiday as one of many you may make to this corner of the world. I remember, when preparing to go on holiday in Barcelona for a long weekend, that we had a list of places we wanted to see that stretched to two Filofax pages. There is seriously that much to do in and around Barcelona.

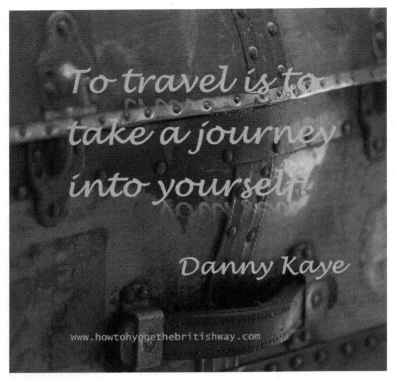

To travel is to take a journey into yourself

Danny Kaye

www.howtohyggethebritishway.com

We could have spent the four days we were there racing around, desperately trying to fit it all in. Instead, we went for the more relaxed approach. There is a very good chance we will make it back to Barcelona, we said, so let's do the things that are top of our list if we can and save the second placers for another time.

We made sure that the Gaudi buildings in the centre of the city got 'done', we took the sight-seeing bus around the harbour and we spent a lot of time walking. A lot of time. Many holidays for my husband and I involve a lot of city walking, because we like cities and you can get a real feel for the place by walking.

We didn't race around, desperate to see everything. There was plenty of time for eating and drinking, for stopping to enjoy the sunshine, and plenty of time to slow down. Did we see everything Barcelona has to offer? No. There's a load of stuff we missed out, but it's still there waiting for us and that's the point. We still have plans for Barcelona.

So how do you go about building hygge into your break?
Make sure you give yourself the gift of time… to relax, to visit, to just be. Don't be a tourist: try to think like a local who is back for a short break in an old and familiar city. I do like my preparation beforehand, to look at the map and websites available and to think, roughly, about what I most want to do. Not plans set in stone, but an idea. I do research what opening times are for the attractions. We once spent an unpleasant Saturday with children in the South Lake District trying to find a tourist attraction open on a Saturday. We ended up at a playground.

And build in time to just be. On a holiday in Paris, when I was alone with two children aged around 10 and 8, we took a whole afternoon off one day. We went to the Place des Vosges in the Marais district, where I sat and read while they played for a couple of hours. With drinks in the bag and an ice cream shop around the corner, we were set. We only moved eventually because we were due to go to the late-night opening at the Louvre and had to meet up with the rest of the family.

I still look back on it as one of my most pleasant afternoons. Do I regret not visiting Victor Hugo's house in the corner? No, not really. I can always go back, and even if I never see the place again I have the memory of a long August day in the shade with my children. They remember a day of freedom and no museum until after tea. It taught me a valuable lesson; sometimes the best days of a holiday are those where you do very little and give yourself permission to just be. Pure hygge.

Take account of your companions. As our children grew, they began to have preferences. Our eldest is happy with museums, exhibitions, anywhere that tells a story. Our second child needs movement, action, adventure. The daughter loves to shop... not to buy, so much as to shop. Any holiday we have has to take account of all of these, as well as the need for rest and recuperation. That can take some doing if the area you visit is lacking in, say, animal attractions. My only advice is do your best. You may need to trade times off against each other and use that valuable skill of blackmail to get them all going the same way at the same time.

Fortunately, there are overlaps. We can always rely on the youngest two to say yes to karting, woodland trails and sports-based activities. Eldest and youngest will visit any place that has a bookshop, while eldest and second will visit mechanical museums. All of them enjoy food, so very often the best bribery has a little fika attached. Very hygge. And animal attractions are always popular, even with our teenagers. Now they're older, we give them responsibility for deciding what to do. Either they look the area up on line and ask about activities, or we look together and they choose from what's available. It does mean we end up going back to places, like the Rabbit Farm we visited twice in one holiday in North Wales, but it makes for less arguments and stress. And less stress will always lead to more hygge.

Of course, that hyggely feeling isn't just for stationary activities. It's entirely possible to feel hyggely when you're being active. A good walk along the beach, a hike up a mountain (hill) or a bike ride along a trail can all be very hyggely. Make sure you have your refreshments sorted, and see Chapter x for more ideas on hygge in the wild.

Finally a word on holiday souvenirs:

Leave nothing but footprints, take nothing but photos. It has taken me years to realise that whatever I buy on holiday has to mean something, to spark joy, or it's just another bit of junk filling up my house. I do still have a fondness for snow-globes. They're small, cheap (relatively) and you can get them nearly everywhere you go. I keep mine on the shelves in the Family room, although they have been used for table decorations at a themed evening and I've used them in school as visual aids in geography.

I also invest in one carefully chosen and meaningful Christmas decoration from each holiday. These really are beautifully hyggely, since they give me the pleasure of choosing one when I'm on holiday (and so remind me of my favourite season of the year) and also remind me of the holiday when I'm putting up the tree. I love putting them on the tree, and thinking of each holiday as I do. Places like Oberammergau are represented with beautiful hand carved wooden decorations, while Paris has a massively gaudy bauble. I love to buy the St Nicholas historical figures decorations, so Portsmouth is represented by Nelson and Hampton Court by Henry VIII. I write the name of the holiday and the year on the back if I can, so I know how long it's been since we visited.

Otherwise, the souvenir shop in most places is only ever used to buy a bar of chocolate if we're low on steam, and that's as a last resort if I haven't remembered to pack something nibbly in my bag. The bowls, vases, boxes or anything else are left behind. I don't need them. They're excess baggage.

Instead, I take masses of photos. Some never get off my computer, but others can be made into memory books of particularly good holidays. There are several good online services that offer this, and often a voucher is available to cut the cost.

Yes, it takes time, but we still have our holiday book from Edinburgh that gives us pleasure. It's easier than scrapbooking as well, since it doesn't take up as much space or need as much equipment.

Your Holiday Homework:

1. What makes a good holiday for you and your family or friends? List the top days you can remember having and see if there's a link between them. Were they active days? Lazy days? Or is food a big thing for you?

2. Panic over getting ready can spoil the hygge of the best holiday. How forward-thinking are you? Do you write lists? Plan menus? Print off tourist information? Perhaps having some packing lists ready on your computer could take some stress away. Begin to compile a skeleton list with the things you know you'll want every time

3. What would your perfect vacation look like? Even if it is monetarily beyond your means at the moment, write down now a description of where and what you would do.

4. Memory is vital for gratitude. Take a moment now and write down your best holiday memories.

When it rains….

I am writing this chapter of the book in April of 2017. In Scotland today, it snowed. In April. My car had icy frost on the roof this morning and I was on the point of getting my big coat out. What's my point? That the weather is awkward and sometimes not very amenable.

The UK weather has a reputation for being unpredictable… that's why we talk about it so much. At any time in the year it can be chilly and wet, there is no rainy season, only a day when it hasn't rained yet, and umbrella sales remain pretty constant throughout the year. We trust and hope it will be good, but realistically expect it will rain at some point in the week. We can watch and plan and hope for a bright sunny day for the trip to the beach… but nothing in life is certain except Death and Taxes.

So, what do you do when the rain starts and the activity you wanted to do looks set to be a wash out?

Go Outside Anyway.

Alfred Wainwright, a great British walker, reckoned the best advice on this quarter came from the Norwegians. There is no such thing as bad weather, only unsuitable clothing.

I can vouch for this, having lived through a good 15 years as the mother of three and spending several long summer holidays watching the rain coming down as the tempers rise. Being outside even if only for a short time is such a chance to release pent up emotion and moods. It's a chance to let off steam, to breathe deeply and to be free.

I like to keep the door open in all weathers during the summer. Even rain. There is something hypnotic about watching the drops racing down the window. We have brollies located at both the front and back door and often use them just to pop out to do what we have to do. A good brolly is so useful, don't you think?

Children love the rain, and rain in the summer can be the best kind. It's wet but not freezing cold. If you go out without a coat or an umbrella, then getting changed and drying clothes off afterwards isn't usually a pain in summer, especially if the rain stops and the sun comes out again. And the atmosphere after summer rain can have a quite distinct smell, very fresh and ionised. There is proof that it smells differently for everyone, and that the scent alters according to location[38]. And the scent of the air just before it rains? That's called petrichor[39], the ethereal blood of stones. Although there's a convoluted scientific explanation now for what makes the smell, at a fundamental level all we need to know is that our ancestors, who relied on rain for their crops and livestock to survive, were tuned into the scent and we modern humans still haven't left the old senses behind.

---

[38] http://science.howstuffworks.com/nature/climate-weather/atmospheric/question479.htm

[39] http://earthsky.org/earth/whats-that-smell-in-the-air-when-its-about-to-rain

Back to the book though… just go and do whatever you were going to do anyway, only wear a mac or carry a brolly. Park walking, beachcombing, even swimming in an outdoor pool can all be done in the rain.

One long lost holiday in my teenage years we were in a caravan site in Germany with an outdoor pool.

The rain had been pretty steady all morning, and after lunch we were fed up. My Mum, in a rare exhibition of giddiness, threw our swimming costumes at us and told us just to get out there and swim. We were the only people in the pool that afternoon, and true enough if we tried to sunbathe or just sit by the side it was chilly enough to make us shiver, but we actually felt warmer in the water, and spent a pleasant hour splashing and swimming lazily about. When we got out, it was straight into the campsite showers and a seat by the barbecue to warm up, though.

I seem to remember we tried this again another day and lasted ten minutes. I think the glowering clouds and the rumble of thunder in the distance drove us out.

Summer thunder can be a fantastic sight. Like all natural phenomenon, the causes are pretty impressive just by themselves, and watching a storm brewing and then discharging all that power is impressive. My Nan was always terrified of thunder and would disconnect the TV, the telephone, the kettle and possibly anything with a plug if she could. Being world-wise teenagers, we used to laugh at her, but there are reports of houses being struck by lightning and appliances blowing up or catching fire[40].

These are, of course, isolated incidents, so I'll half back my Granny and unplug the TV. You'd want to turn it off during a storm anyway. Who would want to miss the fantastic light and sound display put on by Nature? Apart possibly from a brontophobe.

My own children respect storms, but appreciate the display. Catching a look at a bolt of fork lightening as it happens is pretty impressive, and working out how far away the epicentre of the storm is (3 seconds of difference between the lightning and the thunderclap for every mile) is an example of science in very real action. Make cocoa, get the cards out and have a few hyggely moments watching the sky. And when the clouds have cleared and the rain has stopped… get outside. The scent is amazing, and the air positively fizzes.

---

[40] http://stormhighway.com/what_happens_when_lightning_strikes_a_house.php

And you could always visit an indoor activitiy like a museum, cinema, bowling or indoor play area. Having a list of these ready in your mind for a really wet day helps.

Stay indoors and have a Rain Day

If the weather is too bad, or the activity you wanted to do is cancelled or just simply because you really want to, then having a Rain Day is a brilliant thing to do. This works for all ages of humanity, from young to old.

Most rain days start by turning off the TV. The point of a Rain Day is to enjoy the hygge of the situation you're in, not take yourself away to a far-flung part of TV land. The TV will come into its own later, don't worry, but just for now you need to indulge in some here and now mindfulness.

Make a favourite warm drink. Tea or hot chocolate are our favourites, but coffee is good too. I love Earl Grey tea for the summertime, but I'm also fond of chai all year round. Made in a proper teapot and served in proper teacups it can be such a chance to slow down and appreciate the moment. Turn your chair to face the window, and watch. As you sip your drink, watch the drops meander down the window pane. With children, encourage them to trace the drops as they fall. Pick a drop each and let the water run races for you. Look past the window and into the garden or street. What's the rain like? Can you categorise it into heavy or light, intermittent or persistent? Is it a mist of rain, a drizzle of rain, a shower of rain or a downpour?

I love listening to the sound of rain, especially in a proper downpour when it goes lighter and then heavier at intervals. The sudden thumping of myriads of large drops onto a conservatory roof or (lucky you) tin caravan ceiling is rhythmical.

Look at the sky. What colour is it? What are the clouds like? Are they moving or static? Do they make pictures or is the sky glowering? Can you see any blue sky in any direction? One memorable day we stood outside our house (when my daughter was little more than 3) as she proudly proclaimed, "That direction, blue skies, blue skies in that direction, blue skies over there and above us a Big Black Raincloud". It really was like those cartoons where the cloud hovers over one particular spot. Of course, we knew the fact that everywhere else there was blue skies meant it couldn't rain forever. We also hoped, as all people do, that the sun and the rain together would give us a rainbow.

I know that you can explain rainbows away with a scientific explanation about refraction and bending light, but as I love myths and legends of all sorts. I will stick with the Christian myth of it being God's promise to us that he will never again flood the world and wipe us out, or I'll take the Irish legend of the leprechauns. It's fun to try and decide where the pot of gold is, and lovely when you're travelling to realise it must be over your house. My home life is still my treasure.

Back to your rain day. Keep well hydrated with tea or water, and judge when it's time to move away from the window. Watching rain is one of those mindless activities that can often spark deep discussions that need to be had, but never seem to have a natural opportunity. You know, the deep talk about life and purpose, or what school has been like or whether you really love the person you've been dating. I have my best discussions with the teenage sons when we're doing something side by side like this. It's like the inside version of the fire pit. Water and fire, see? Two sides of the meditation imagery.

LET THE RAIN KISS YOU. LET THE RAIN BEAT UPON YOUR HEAD WITH SILVER LIQUID DROPS. LET THE RAIN SING YOU A LULLABY.

LANGSTON HUGHES

www.howtohyggethebritishway.com

When the watching ceases to feel relaxing, stop. Everybody has a different threshold for watching rather than moving. Some people can stay still for hours, others need to shift position after a few minutes. You're aiming to feel relaxed, not bored.

My default Rain Day activity is a craft. I love crochet, so I can always sit and hook away at a blanket, a shawl, or other crochet project. Usually I have my Thinking Project and an easier, mindless project that requires nothing more complicated than counting sets of trebles and a turn at the end of the row. Rain Days are mindless crochet days.

You could do painting, model making, writing, drawing, hama beads, clay or anything that you enjoy and can lose time in. The point is, rather like the rain drops, to lose yourself in the flow. It isn't even to create something so much as to create. You can put all the hama beads back before ironing them, or crumple the clay at the end. It's the process that you're after on a Rain Day. I think you'd be surprised at what you make, though. That time spent already resting and enjoying acts as a powerful creative tool very often. If your preconceived ideas have been cleared from your brain, the creativity has space to come in. Don't look for it, just let it come. And if you're not a creator, then read a book. A real book, with paper pages. A Rain Day calls for you to indulge your senses fully. I am a mad Kindle fan, but I know that on a day like this I need to find my comfort book, possibly Meik Wiking's Little Book of Hygge or one of Nigella Lawson's recipe books.

If the day is too dark for your activity, light a candle. Light a few, and enjoy the feeling of being electricity free for a while. With children, I'd advise you to use tealights in good jars that keep the flame well away from fiddling fingers and never to leave them unattended.

Children love to craft and make things. You may find if you're at home with them that your craft has to take a back seat. I apologise, but there will be days for finishing your projects when they're older. For now, you get down to their level and build the track, play with the Lego, paint the colouring book.

Is it lunchtime? Or time for afternoon tea? Make up a small tray with food. Biscuits, finger sandwiches of cucumber or salmon (if you have any in) or cakes can all be delicious. Use some of the trapped time to make a cake or scones. A good basic scone recipe is easy enough for a child to learn and eaten warm from the oven with jam or butter is a paradise on Earth.

Keep food simple and have a carpet picnic made up of finger foods. At lunchtime or for supper it can be fun to eat together on the floor, especially if you, like we used to, eat most of your meals *en famille* at the table. Chicken wings, or popcorn chicken, cocktail sausages, bread with pate or cheese, a pizza cut up, chips, crisps, vegetable strips and dips. Keep the meal easy to make and easy to eat. The Rain Day is a lazy day, a chance for you to enjoy being rather than doing.

With adults, a bottle of cold cider or beer is the finishing touch, but for children drinking anything through a straw will be a big treat (in my house, it would be coke drunk from the mason jar glasses that were so big a couple of years ago) and it might be worth making strawberry milk shakes using strawberries, a banana, yoghurt, and ice blended together to give a thick consistency.

And, if you can, finish off the day with a walk around the neighbourhood straight after the rain stops. Smell it, enjoy the shine of the wet pavements, splash in the puddles, appreciate what a gift rain is. Sometimes I think people who live in temperate regions like the UK are so spoiled by having regular rainfall that we forget to honour it as the life-giving force it is.

Of course, if the rain is set for the night and not going to let you walk, you can always chicken out. Switch on the TV, put in a DVD or film and have a movie night. With the lights off and curtains closed, seats put in a row and a half term serving of popcorn or ice cream, it's a happy end to a happy day.

Bake together or on your own.

Kitchen alchemy is a wonderful thing, if you're good at it. Taking a variety of ingredients and transforming them into cakes or cookies is sheer magic, and makes very good use of a wet afternoon. The scents also make the house smell beautiful.

I love baking, but I've lost the keys to the kitchen; since my daughter hit 11 I have been very much the junior partner in her culinary adventures. I buy the materials, she chooses what to make and asks me only occasionally to help. I'm not complaining. Lemon drizzle cake is gorgeous whichever way it comes to me. The fact I don't have to make it is, to me, an advantage.

Sarah has a fascination with colours in cakes. I bought myself a set of Wilton paste food colouring pots, as recommended by Yarnstorm[41] blog years ago, only to find that she took to them like a duck to water. She loves the blues and greens of life, so rather disconcertingly you can have a plain cake in any of those colours. Very often her cakes come marbled with chocolate and purple as well. They taste divine, but look amazing.

She uses a basic cake recipe and adapts it to suit her purposes. I call it the Football Cake, since the ratio goes 4:4:4:2 (if you use imperial measurements)

---

[41] http://yarnstorm.blogs.com/ Written by Jane Brocket, whose books are sadly now out of print but made me very happy when first out. She was a knitter, a textile artist and a baker supreme. Her blog archives make a great starting point for anyone who wants inspiration on how to use the Domestic Arts well in their life.

Sarah's Football Cake Recipe

4oz butter

4oz caster sugar

4oz self-raising flour

2 eggs

A splash of milk

1tsp vanilla extract

A dab of food colouring paste.

(1oc cocoa powder if you want a chocolate cake)

Method

1. Butter and/or line a baking tin. This makes an 8inch round tin cake that is quite thin. Preheat the oven to GM4 (180 deg C or 350 deg F)

2. Using the all-in-one method, use a hand whisk to mix the butter, sugar, flour and eggs altogether (if you're making a chocolate cake, add the 1oz of cocoa powder instead of 1oz of flour).

3. Add the other ingredients and stir well.

4. Put into the baking tin and bake for 25 minutes. Test by gently patting the top. If your fingerprint bounces back, the cake is well on its way to being cooked. If an inserted skewer comes out clean, it is cooked and can be taken out of the oven. It may take up to 30 or 35 minutes for this. Different ovens have different temperatures, actually, so do please do what you know works for you.

5. Turn out onto a wire rack to cool and then decorate with icing or sweets.

Rainy Day Resources

It's worth being prepared if you're a mother, or even if you're not. On a rainy day it can be a real mood boost if you can reach for a box or basket of stuff that you only ever use when the weather is keeping you inside. In his book, The Little Book of Hygge, Meik Wiking suggests assembling a hygge box, with the things you need to enable hygge even on a dark, horrible day. I'm suggesting the summer equivalent.

When my children were little, I had a small wicker chest. It lived in the Family Room and only came out in times of emergency. It had a couple of their favourite picture books, a pack of Very Special Grown Up Felt Pens, a colouring book, stickers, sequins, hama beads and some glue. At various times I added sweets or sultanas and sometimes a homemade voucher for ice cream or popcorn. On the worst wet days of the year, we used to get the chest out, and just make stuff.

There is nothing to say you can't make a grown-up equivalent. Put in some adult colouring pages, if that's hygge for you, a couple of sachets of posh hot chocolate, a packet of Love Hearts or Parma Violet sweets, some tea bags, a special summertime mug, this month's copy of your favourite magazine saved for just such a day, a book that you want to read or want to read again and some scented tealights.

Usually, I'm not a big scented candle fan but on a dark, miserable day a candle that fills the house with the fragrance of lavender or strawberries will help you to make believe that you're out in the fields, even if you're not.

Add a small miniature of which ever tipple tickles your fancy. I have a hankering for some Valencia Orange flavoured gin, but I need a willing friend to purchase it for me as a present. I can imagine that sitting sipping gin as the weather dances to its own tune outside would be very therapeutic. Or using 3 tablespoons to make a gin and tonic loaf cake[42] to eat as you create.

Keep the box or bag safe until the weather turns and you can just casually pull it out, feeling all satisfied that even a wet day is an opportunity for a hyggely moment for you.

---

[42] http://www.goodhousekeeping.co.uk/food/recipes/gin-and-tonic-loaf

Your Rainy Day Homework:

1. List the venues near you that are worth visiting on a rainy day.

2. Have you ever enjoyed a rain day? What did you do? What feelings did you have? What resources did you use? Looking at enjoyment in the past helps us to find enjoyment in the present.

3. Write a list here of the things you would put in your Rainy Day box. Find a small, but beautiful, box or basket and start collecting them.

Indoor hygge in the heat

Anyone who has ever had the pain of looking after a little child in the middle of a heatwave knows how horrible heat can be. And for some people it doesn't have to be so hot to be too hot. I am not a natural heat-lover. I would far rather put on my hat, scarf and gloves and walk in the snow than do pretty much anything in any sort of heat above 20 degrees C. I am a wuss. So when the heat rises outside and it's too warm to even think of going outside, creating hygge seems like an impossible dream. It isn't.... but it will require a change of your mind set. Hygge is about appreciating small things, of finding a comforting thought in any situation. The middle of the hottest day in the year is a good time to turn all Pollyanna for your own sake. Now, this is a really hard instruction but you must do it, or no good can come of anything else.

Stop complaining. Not even a little whimper.

Heat is horrible, yes, but the more you talk about how hot/humid/horrible it is, the more your brain will think it is hot/horrible/humid and tell your body to respond in kind.

You are going to have to play tricks with your brain. Keep saying positive things like, "It's lovely to see the Sun again today. Imagine how brown my arms will be. Gosh, it's not as cold as yesterday.". Yes, I know it sounds silly, but it does actually work.

And on the hottest, most humid day of the year, you need to stay indoors. You need to find ways to keep out of the heat, keep in the shade and keep your shade cool.

Use the House well.

You need to look at the home you're in and work out how the Sun and heat affect it. Which side of the house are the main rooms on? Where does the sun rise? Which windows get the most sun? Which get the least?

In the Northern hemisphere, the sun shines predominantly on the South side of houses. That's why kitchens and larders were usually designed to be on the Northern, darker side of the house, so that the sun didn't heat them up and cause things to spoil quicker. In the modern days of refrigeration, we no longer really bother about that. Our modern fridge-freezer will keep our drink cold even if the sun shines on it all day. That's all well and good for the iced tea you've made, but we humans need to think back to the olden days to keep our cool as well.

My own home is very lucky: it has the front door facing North and the living room facing South. In the wintertime, the sun streams in for the best part of the day and heats the room up a little more. In the summer, the sun beats down relentlessly (I wish) onto the patio flags outside and keeps the area just inside the French windows at a constant sweltering in a heat wave. Even with the doors and windows open and the curtains mostly closed to keep the room dark, in a heatwave it feels sweltering.

We're fortunate to have a Family Room as well. It's a converted garage and it leads off the kitchen at the front of the house. In other words, it's on the North side. Yes, the sun hits it…. eventually… but for most of the day the room is in the shadow of the house. With open windows and a fan if necessary it can be a fair bit cooler than the rest of the house. When the children were little, we actually did use the two living areas as a summer room and a winter room. The same things that keep the Family Room cool in summer, keep it freezing in winter.

So how do you go about heat-proofing your home? Well, there is always air conditioning which I know is a necessity for many people in warmer places. It's costly to install and can be costly to run, so it's only really an option if the heat of your home is always too great to do anything.

(On an environmental note, if you do use air conditioning, try turning the thermostat up a couple of degrees. You don't need a house that feels like a fridge, what you need is a house that hits you as cooler than the outside. Turning it down will also use less energy, so it's cheaper)

If you don't have air conditioning and don't want to use it, you need to look at other ways to maintain your cool.

Look at your rooms and see which way your main living area faces. How many windows are there in your living area? Windows will trap heat and make the room feel warmer, like in a greenhouse. It is possible to cut down a rise in temperature due to windows simply by having and using blinds or curtains. Anything that blocks the light from entering through the glass will stop the temperature rising. Fit the kind of blinds that suit your style. We have venetian blinds in the office, and they are a Godsend when the sun shines down on me in my little glass pen. Choose wisely and the blinds will outlast you, possibly. Even thick net curtains will create a barrier to the heat coming in and help cool the room down. We actually just pull the curtains across for most of the day, and then open them in the evening. No, we don't see the garden, but we do get a cooler living space.

And close the doors to rooms you're not using on the sunny side. If you have south facing bedrooms, they are going to be little greenhouses of heat. Closing off the door stops that heat getting through to the rest of the house.

Conversely, in the evening open the doors and let the cool get into those rooms as well.

Fake air conditioning with a bowl of iced water or solid ice block carefully positioned with a fan angled to bounce air off it and into the room. If your fan has a grill cover, you can also place a damp (not wet) cloth over it to get a cooling effect. Replace the cloth often as the water will soon dry up.

You can try this on a larger scale with dampened towels or sheets hung over opened windows to encourage damper, cooler air circulating.

Choose your activities carefully

This will not be the day to have a mad race around the house, or to snuggle under Granny's crocheted blanket drinking hot chocolate. It may not even be a day to get dressed in much more than swimming trunks or vest and shorts. I know my babies used to spend a long time every summer dressed just in their nappies... anything else was just too warm for them and me to look at!

You want to be thinking about the three basics of cooling down:

- Shade
- Water
- Cool things to eat and drink

Shade: Keeping curtains closed, or covering very hot windows will help in the house, but on really hot days I used to like using a cotton sheet and setting up an indoor gazebo. This was essentially just a top sheet tied at all four sides to a convenient chair or handle. Keep the sides open, and aim the fan through the tent. We used to crash out on a pile of cushions or towels and read, draw or just sleep the heat away.

Water: Let's face it, children of all ages like water play, and water works well as a cooling agent. I like using the misting bottles that are available for plants or designed for use in hairdressers' shops. I have used these very happily in Nursery schools, filled with water and sprayed above the children to give them a mist of cooling water. Have one in the fridge and spray it in the hottest heat to give the room a cooling mist. You can also spray it into the path of a fan and it will be blown around the room slightly to cool it.

For a more grown up take on water play, try a washing up bowl of water with a few drops of peppermint essence added. Soak your feet in it while sipping a lemonade or elderflower cordial, and enjoy spa treatment at home. Make it even hyggier by listening to your favourite records, or reading a book as you relax.

Cooling things to Eat and Drink: Look up recipes online to make smoothies or slushies. Anything involving crushed ice is good to eat in the heat, as is plenty of cooled water although surprisingly the best thing to drink to actually cool the body down is a hot drink.

This triggers the sweat reflex and sweating is the body's main physiological method of keeping cool.

A member of the Hygge Nook described her perfect ways to keep cool in a list:

- keeping a gallon of iced tea in the fridge for the afternoons
- collecting, making and eating lots of new salad recipes
- sitting in front of a fan while soaking your feet in a tub of cold water infused with peppermint or rose essential oils
- sipping lots of water (with slices of lemon, lime or cucumber in it)

It's recommended that you don't drink too much in the heat. Alcohol acts as a diuretic, so it dehydrates the body. Keeping the body hydrated helps with that sweating response we spoke of earlier, so you want to be filling up your body with good liquid, not clearing it out too quickly. That said, a cool beer drunk in the middle of the afternoon on a warm Sunday isn't going to kill you.

Eat Seasonally: Eat Light

Making the most of good, seasonal food is common sense in the summertime. I find my menu plan lightens up considerably when the sun is beating down and I lack both the time and the desire to stand cooking in the kitchen for ages.

In a really good summer my oven possibly stays off from one week's end to the next. Instead of roasts or bakes or slow cooked casseroles, we eat a lot more quickly prepared stir fries using a rainbow of vegetables, salads served with simple grilled chicken or beef and more fresh fruit and veg than during the winter. It just feels right to make the most of the glorious bounty available.

It's worth having a few different salad recipes in mind, so that at any time you can use courgettes, cauliflower, spinach, rocket, tomatoes and cucumbers in a variety of ways. And it's worth having a few meat glazes to hand as well, so that the plain chicken breast doesn't lose its appeal.

On the hottest of hot days you won't feel like cooking at all. That's fine. Open a tin of tuna or mackerel, slice some vegetables, cut a couple of pieces of bread each and eat a cold meal. Or put off cooking until the sun has set and you feel cooler. Part of the fun of summer is the freedom to change your routine. Our ancestors knew that, they knew they had to work while the sun shone, so their food was easy, grab and go. Look for inspiration to those earlier times. Perhaps try a raw vegetarian diet for a day or two, with no cooking at all. Or, if you must have hot things, use the slow cooker instead of the oven to make chilli, Bolognese or even to roast meat. It will generate a lot less heat, and you can leave it to work in the kitchen while you go out to work or for a day out.

Ploughman's lunch makes an excellent midday meal. Ham, cheese, pickle, bread and an apple are enough for lunch for anyone. Forget the plastic versions cafes used to offer. Visit a local farmer's market or stop off at a stall on an excursion and treat yourself to fresh cheese from the manufacturer, some home-made pickle and a loaf of artisan bread. With a glass of wine or a cool beer, it's a feast fit for a king! And it doesn't generate a lot of washing up.

Your Indoor Hygge in the Heat Homework:

1. If it's really that hot, you won't want to do anything. Strip off as far as is decent, spray yourself with a fine mist of water now and again and appreciate the heat.

Afterword, or, what you will.

So, there you go. A whole book on how to hygge when the sun shines. I hope it's got you thinking about what hygge really means to you, and away from the idea of just putting it into the blanket box along with the thick throws and warm fires.

Hygge has to mean so much more than just a pretty picture to make sense. Human beings are built to live in groups, and those groups need to learn how to spend time together in all sorts of weather. Our ancestors had no choice but to get along most of the time. We've grown so used to having an individual life, with TV, phone and food when we want it and increasingly consumed alone. Hygge is a useful break in that lifestyle. It's a reminder that we are still at heart that man from the Dark Ages who needed his community to survive, we're still the medieval woman gathering her crops and making a meal to share, we're still the people who went through the whole of history scrimping and saving and learning how to make the best of everything.

As the summer heat grows, I hope that we can grow together and appreciate freedom to spend time together in a way that strengthens our friendship and trust of one another.

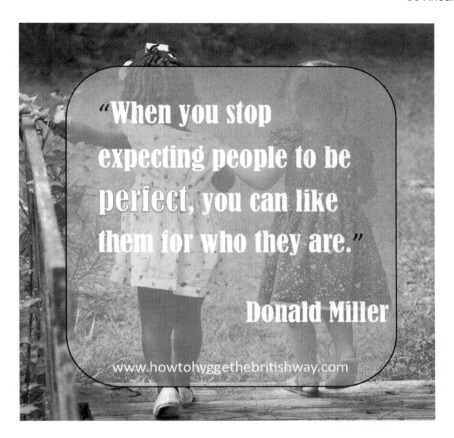

"When you stop expecting people to be perfect, you can like them for who they are."

Donald Miller

www.howtohyggethebritishway.com

And, for the final words, a quote from another Hygge Nook member:

I am an Australian. We have no choice but to adapt hygge to the warmer weather for many months of the year. Here are some of my favourites: Open the windows first thing to let the cool of the mornings come through; wear flowy ,beautiful maxi dresses; drink icy cold beer or ginger ale on a balcony enjoying the sea breeze if your lucky; bbq with friends; take your dog to the beach; yoga outdoors; swing in a hammock under a shady tree; find a summer scent that smells a little tropical; fruit salad; enjoy an icypole or a slushie; walk at dawn; eat your dinner later in the day; spread strong plastic on a grassy hill, pour on some dish detergent and run a hose over it for your kids to slide down; sleep under the stars in a swag or in a tent. Let me know if you want me to keep going.

This is the way of my life.

Summer Resources

Good books for inspiration

These books aren't actually about hygge at all. A lot of hygge books I've read actually make very little fuss about hygge in the summer, and concentrate mostly on the throws and candles side. Of course, there are exceptions like Meik Wiking's Little Book of Hygge that had a chapter on hygge through the year, or Signe Johanssen's How to Hygge which has to take summer hygge into account, since it's all about getting outside and living well. These books are just a few that I found useful in my life-long quest for things to do and be happy with. And they're in no particular order.

Stories in the Stars: An Atlas of Constellations: Susanna Hislop
The Barbecue! Bible: Steven Kauchlich
BBQ: Jamie Oliver
Spirals in Time: Helen Scales

The Photographic Recognition Guide to Seashells of the World: from the Smithsonian

Gift From the Sea: Anne Morrow Lindbergh

The Wonderful Weekend Book: Elspeth Thompson

The Gentle Art of Domesticity: Jane Brockett (out of print)

Cherry Cakes and Ginger Beer: Jane Brockett (out of print)

A Home for All Seasons: Kristen Perers (out of print)

Great sites to look up

Again, just a few of the sites I found useful in researching this book. God help me if I ever get around to writing a proper text book. The writing and editing part's the easy part... remembering what references I used and finding the resources is by far the hardest part for me! If you have any favourite sites and resources, do pop by The Hygge Nook and let me know. These are in no order at all.

https://www.bookbarninternational.com/ This bookshop in a barn has a café that gets really good reviews. Have I been? No, but I'd love to know is it as good as it looks?

https://thefuntimesguide.com/summer-fun-activities-for-adults/ I love the idea of putting on masking tape before sunbathing to get stripes! Mad ideas… but lots of fun.

https://uk.pinterest.com/ Has there ever been a better place to find ideas for anything and everything? Just search 'summer fun' and see what you get

Your local city events page: If you're lucky, there should be lots of things happening that you may never even have thought of. Get out there and explore…

https://www.gov.uk/government/publications/the-countryside-code The official government page for The Countryside Code. It's available to download from here, or there are links to an online version as well.

https://www.airbnb.co.uk/ or the USA equivalent. I like looking at this just to see inside the houses and apartments of different countries. One day, I promise myself, one day I will make it to Copenhagen and stay in an apartment there….

A Useful Outdoor Summer Activities Basket:

There are things I've found useful over the years for keeping children and adults entertained in and out of the garden.

It might be an idea to keep a backpack or basket ready in the back of the car so that, at a moment's notice, you can throw a picnic together, grab a bottle of fluid and get on your way. Rather like a mother keeps the nappy bag ready at all times.

- Wet wipes or nappy wipes (you can get biodegradable ones)
- Kitchen roll or packet of tissues
- Plastic beakers
- Small ball eg tennis ball
- Frisbee
- Pack of cards
- Sharp knife for food
- Penknife
- A couple of binbags
- Elastic bands
- Oilcloth squares for sitting on.
- Torch
- Small food bags (for shell collections, leaves, flowers etc.
- A copy of the Countryside Code (there is a downloadable bookmark that you could print off and laminate)

Thank you for reading. If you've enjoyed the book and found parts of it useful, please let me know via Amazon or Goodreads by leaving a good review. If you didn't like it, I'd like to know that as well. Criticism, good and bad, is useful.

With love,

Jo x

Jo Kneale will return in

How to Hygge Your Christmas

Available on Amazon in paperback and ebook version
sometime this Autumn.
Or
In December if she doesn't get her act
together and get the book written in time!